Cycle Tours

21 one-day routes in

East Anglia

North

Compiled by
Nick Cotton

PHILIP'S

Contents

On-road routes

Back cover photograph: near Burnham Overy

Off-road routes

First published 1998 by

Ordnance Survey and George Philip Ltd, an imprint of
Romsey Road   Reed Consumer Books Ltd
Maybush   Michelin House
Southampton   81 Fulham Road
SO16 4GU   London SW3 6RB

Text and compilation
Copyright © George Philip Ltd 1998
Maps Copyright © Crown Copyright 1998

The route maps in this book are based upon Ordnance Survey® Landranger® mapping.

The cross-profile diagrams in this book have been created using Ordnance Survey® Land-Form PANORAMA™ Digital height data.

Ordnance Survey and Landranger are registered trade marks and Land-Form PANORAMA is a trade mark of Ordnance Survey, the National Mapping Agency of Great Britain.

First edition 1998

A catalogue record for this atlas is available from the British Library

ISBN 0 600 59219 7
Printed in Spain

Acknowledgements
AA Photo Library 49, 68, 99, 105, 141, 142 • Nick Cotton 79, 89, 100, 121, 127, 133, 135 • Derek Forss 36, 85, 115 • Judy Todd 23, 29, 46, 56, 61, 73, 96, 129

• edited by Bill Hemsley, Tracy Hunt and Sandy Sims • designed by James Hughes • picture research by Jenny Faithfull • production by Joanna Walker

Portions of Places of Interest text are derived from The Reader's Digest Association Limited Touring Guide to Britain © 1998

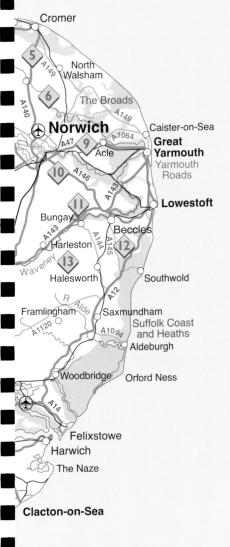

Cromer

North
Walsham

The Broads

Norwich

Caister-on-Sea

**Great
Yarmouth**

Yarmouth
Roads

Acle

Lowestoft

Bungay

Beccles

Harleston

Southwold

Halesworth

Framlingham

Saxmundham

Suffolk Coast
and Heaths

Aldeburgh

Woodbridge

Orford Ness

Felixstowe

Harwich

The Naze

Clacton-on-Sea

Key to routes
Legend

 On-road cycle route

 Off-road cycle route

 Motorway, service area

Junction, limited access

A31   Primary route

A684   Other main road

🏰 **Dover**   City / major town

○ Mere   Primary town

○ Yate   Other town

Primary routes form a national network of
recommended through routes which
complement the motorway system

The primary towns shown on this map appear
on traffic signs which, on primary routes, have a
green background or, on motorways, have a blue
background

County boundary

National boundary

- - - - -   Domestic ferry route

Passenger railway

✈ ✈   Airport / with customs

(H)   Heliport

National parks, forest
parks and areas of
scenic beauty

Scale 1:1 000 000 1 cm to 10 km or about 1 inch to 16 miles

Quick reference chart

Route	Page	Distance (kilometres)	Grade (easy/moderate/strenuous)[1]	Links with other routes[1]	Tourist information centres[2]

On-road routes

Route	Page	Distance	Grade	Links	Tourist information centres
1 Across northwest Norfolk from Sandringham to Burnham Market	16	54	🖊	2,4	Hunstanton 01485 532610
2 North from Fakenham to the coast at Wells-next-the-Sea	22	50	🖊	1,3,4	Fakenham 01328 851981
3 Northeast from Fakenham to the coast at Blakeney and Cley	28	66	🖊	2,4,7,8	Fakenham 01328 851981
4 Southwest from Fakenham to Castle Acre	36	56	🖊	2,3,8	Fakenham 01328 851981
5 North from Aylsham to the coast at Cromer	42	55	🖊	6	Cromer 01263 512497
6 From Aylsham to Wroxham, in the heart of the Norfolk Broads	48	56	🖊	5,9	Hoveton* 01603 782281
7 From Swaffham to Cockley Cley, the Nar Valley and Castle Acre	54	55	🖊	4	King's Lynn 01553 763044
8 North from East Dereham to Colkirk and the Wensum Valley	60	50	🖊	2,3,4	Norwich 01603 666071
9 Southeast from Wroxham to the River Yare at Reedham	66	60	🖊	6	Hoveton* 01603 782281
10 Along the Yare valley from Norwich to Loddon	72	51	🖊	11	Norwich 01603 666071
11 The marshlands of the River Waveney northeast of Bungay	78	55	🖊	10, 12	Beccles* 01502 713196
12 Southeast from Beccles to the coast at Southwold	84	51	🖊	11	Southwold* 01502 724729
13 From Harleston through the 'Saints' to Laxfield and Hoxne	90	60	🖊		Diss 01379 650523

[1]**Links with other routes** Use this information to create a more strenuous ride or if you are planning to do more than one ride in a day or on a weekend or over a few days. The rides do not necessarily join: there may be a distance of about 5 km (3 miles) between the closest points. Some routes share the same starting point, which may be a good place to base yourself for a weekend.

Where possible, adjacent rides, and suggested links to them, are highlighted on the route mapping by a narrow yellow line and identified by the appropriate route number symbol.

[2]**Tourist Information Centres** You can contact them for details about accommodation. If they cannot help, there are many books that recommend places to stay. If nothing is listed for the place where you want to stay, try phoning the post office or the pub in the village to see if they can suggest somewhere.

*Tourist Information Centres marked with an asterisk are open from Easter to the end of September only

East Anglia – North

East Anglia is a region of easy familiarity rather than big, dramatic surprises: gently undulating arable land, clumps of broadleaf trees, flint churches, old thatched red-brick houses and barns, the sandy forestry plantations of Breckland and the dark rich soil of the Fenland. The topography, with the land never rising to more than around 100 m (330 feet) and the wide visibility on the open lanes, make this sociable, conversational cycling country.

The nature of the region and the distribution of its byway and bridleway network means that the balance of road and offroad rides is tipped in favour of an exploration by lane rather than track. The five offroad rides cover a waymarked route in Thetford Forest and the linear routes of the Peddars Way to the west and the Marriotts Way and Weavers Way in the east.

Thetford Forest offers many miles of fine, well-drained forestry tracks: with a compass and the most up-to-date Ordnance Survey map it should be possible to devise dozens of your own routes. The ride described in the book is a route waymarked by the Forestry Commission. Peddars Way is a 50-mile linear route from Bridgham Heath, east of Thetford up to the coast at Holme-next-the-Sea. It runs along the course of a road built by the Romans in the first century AD and uses a mixture of lanes and tracks. The route described is the bridle route, the course of which differs slightly from that of the Long Distance Footpath. The second linear route, the Marriotts Way, leaves the heart of Norwich and links two separate railway paths.

As for the road rides, the sixteen routes cover over 500 miles of quiet lanes from the Fenland in the west to the coast at Cromer in the north and Southwold in the east. With the exception of the ride from the magnificent cathedral in Ely into the dark and richly fertile surrounding fenland, almost all the other rides link directly or lie within a few miles of another route.

Several towns and villages stand out as good bases from which to explore the surrounding area. Castle Acre is a delightful red-brick and flint village in the northwest corner of the region. The attractive market towns of Swaffham, Fakenham and Aylsham are all starting points for rides to the north and west of Norwich, as are Diss, Bungay and Beccles to the south and east. The nearest Tourist Information Centres are listed in the Quick Reference Chart: they can provide invaluable advice about where to stay.

Abbreviations and instructions

Instructions are given as concisely as possible to make them easy to follow while you are cycling. Remember to read one or two instructions ahead so that you do not miss a turning. This is most likely to occur when you have to turn off a road on which you have been riding for a fairly long distance and these junctions are marked **Easy to miss** to warn you.

If there appears to be a contradiction between the instructions and what you actually see, always refer to the map. There are many reasons why over the course of a few years instructions will need updating as new roads are built and priorities and signposts change.

If giving instructions for road routes is at times difficult, doing so for off-road routes can often be almost impossible, particularly when the route passes through woodland. With few signposts and buildings by which to orientate yourself, more attention is paid to other features, such as gradient and surface. Most of these routes have been explored between late spring and early autumn and the countryside changes its appearance very dramatically in winter. If in doubt, consult your map and check your compass to see that you are heading in the right direction.

Where I have encountered mud I have mentioned it, but this may change, not only from summer to winter but also from dry to wet weather, at any time during the year. At times you may have to retrace your steps and find a road alternative.

Some routes have small sections that follow footpaths. The instructions will highlight these sections where you must get off and push your bike. You may only ride on bridleways and by-ways so be careful if you stray from the given routes.

Directions

L	left
LH	left-hand
RH	right-hand
SA	straight ahead or straight across
bear L or R	make less than a 90-degree (right-angle) turn at a fork in the road or track or at a sharp bend so that your course appears to be straight ahead; this is often written as *in effect SA*
sharp L or R turn	is more acute than 90 degrees
sharp R/L back on yourself	an almost U-turn
sharp LH/RH bend	a 90-degree bend
R then L or R	the second turning is visible then immediately L from the first
R then 1st L	the second turning may be some distance from the first; the distance may also be indicated: *R, then after 1 mile L*

Junctions

T-j	T-junction, a junction where you have to give way
X-roads	crossroads, a junction where you may or may not have to give way
offset X-roads	the four roads are not in the form of a perfect cross and you will have to turn left then right, or vice versa, to continue the route

Signs

'Placename 2'	words in quotation marks are those that appear on signposts; the numbers indicate distance in miles unless stated otherwise
NS	not signposted
trig point	a trigonometrical station

Instructions

An example of an easy instruction is:

4 At the T-j at the end of Smith Road by the White Swan PH R on Brown Street 'Greentown 2, Redville 3'.

There is more information in this instruction than you would normally need, but things do change: pubs may close down and signs may be replaced, removed or vandalized.

An example of a difficult instruction is:

8 Shortly after the brow of the hill, soon after passing a telephone box on the right next L (NS).

As you can see, there is no T-junction to halt you in your tracks, no signpost indicating where the left turn will take you, so you need to have your wits about you in order not to miss the turning.

Fact boxes

The introduction to each route includes a fact box giving useful information:

Start

This is the suggested start point coinciding with instruction 1 on the map. There is no reason why you should not start at another point if you prefer.

Distance and grade

The distance is, of course, that from the beginning to the end of the route. If you wish to shorten the ride, however, the maps enable you to do so.

The number of drinks bottles indicates the grade:

Easy

Moderate

Strenuous

Page diagrams

The on-road routes usually occupy four pages of mapping each. The page diagrams on the introductory pages show how the map pages have been laid out, how they overlap and if any inset maps have been used.

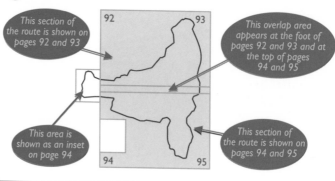

This section of the route is shown on pages 92 and 93

This overlap area appears at the foot of pages 92 and 93 and at the top of pages 94 and 95

This area is shown as an inset on page 94

This section of the route is shown on pages 94 and 95

The grade is based on the amount of climbing involved.

Remember that conditions may vary dramatically with the weather and seasons, especially along off-road sections

Terrain

This brief description of the terrain may be read in conjunction with the cross-profile diagram at the foot of the page to help you to plan your journey.

Nearest railway

This is the distance to the nearest station from the closest point on the route, not necessarily from the start. Before starting out you should check with British Rail for local restrictions regarding the carrying of bicycles.

Refreshments

Pubs and teashops on or near the route are listed. The tankard symbols indicate pubs particularly liked by the author.

Before you go

Preparing yourself

Fitness

Cycling uses muscles in a different way from walking or running, so if you are beginning or returning to it after a long absence you will need time to train your muscles and become accustomed to sitting on a saddle for a few hours. Build up your fitness and stamina gradually and make sure you are using a bicycle that is the right size for you and suits your needs.

Equipment

Attach the following items to the bike: bell, pump, light-brackets and lights, lock-holder and lock, rack and panniers or elastic straps for securing things to the rack, map holder. Unless it is the middle of summer and the weather is guaranteed to be fine, you will need to carry extra clothes, particularly a waterproof, with you, and it is well worth investing in a rack for this purpose.

Wearing a small pouch around your waist is the easiest and safest way of carrying small tools and personal equipment. The basics are: Allen keys to fit the various Allen bolts on your bike, chainlink extractor, puncture repair kit, reversible screwdriver (slot and crosshead), small adjustable spanner, spare inner tube, tyre levers (not always necessary with mountain bike tyres), coins and a phonecard for food and telephone calls, compass.

Additional tools for extended touring: bottom bracket extractor, cone spanners, freewheel extractor, headset spanners, lubricant, socket spanner for pedals, spare cables, spoke-key.

Clothing

What you wear when you are cycling should be comfortable, allowing you, and most especially your legs, to move freely. It should also be practical, so that it will keep you warm and dry if and when the weather changes.

Feet You can cycle in just about any sort of footwear, but bear in mind that the chain has oil on it, so do not use your very best shoes. Leather tennis shoes or something similar, with a smooth sole to slip into the pedal and toe clip are probably adequate until you buy specialist cycling shoes, which have stiffer soles and are sometimes designed for use with specialist pedals.

Legs Cycling shorts or padded cycling underwear worn under everyday clothing make long rides much more comfortable. Avoid tight, non-stretch trousers, which are very uncomfortable for cycling and will sap your energy, as they restrict the movement of your legs; baggy tracksuit bottoms, which can get caught in the chain and will sag around your ankles if they get wet. Almost anything else will do, though a pair of stretch leggings is probably best.

- **Upper body** What you wear should be long enough to cover your lower back when you are leaning forward and, ideally, should have zips or buttons that you can adjust to regulate your temperature. Several thin layers are better than one thick layer.

- **Head** A helmet may protect your head in a fall.

- **Wet weather** A waterproof, windproof top is essential if it looks like rain. A dustbin bag would be better than nothing but obviously a breathable waterproof material is best.

- **Cold weather** A hat that covers your ears, a scarf around your neck, a pair of warm gloves and a thermal top and bottom combined with what you would normally wear cycling should cover almost all conditions.

- **Night and poor light** Wearing light-coloured clothes or reflective strips is almost as important as having lights on your bike. Reflective bands worn around the ankles are particularly effective in making you visible to motorists.

Preparing your bicycle

- You may not be a bicycle maintenance expert, but you should make sure that your bike is roadworthy before you begin a ride.

- If you are planning to ride in soft, off-road conditions, fit fat, knobbly tyres. If you are using the bike around town or on a road route, fit narrower, smoother tyres.

- Check the tyres for punctures or damage and repair or replace if necessary or if you are in any doubt. Keep tyres inflated hard (recommended pressures are on the side wall of the tyre) for mainly on-road riding. You do not need to inflate tyres as hard for off-road use; slightly softer tyres give some cushioning and get better traction in muddy conditions.

- Ensure that the brakes work efficiently. Replace worn cables and brake blocks.

- The bike should glide along silently. Tighten and adjust any part that is loose or rubbing against a moving part. Using a good-quality bike oil lubricate the hubs, bottom bracket, pedals where they join the cranks, chain and gear-changing mechanism from both sides. If the bike still makes grating noises, replace the bearings.

- Adjust the saddle properly. The saddle height should ensure that your legs are working efficiently: too low and your knees will ache; too high and your hips will be rocking in order for your feet to reach the pedals. Some women find the average bike saddle uncomfortable because the female pelvis is a different shape from the male pelvis and needs a broader saddle for support. Some manufacturers make saddles especially for women.

Cross-profiles

The introduction to each route includes a cross-profile diagram. The blue grid indicates 1-kilometre horizontal intervals and 50-metre vertical intervals

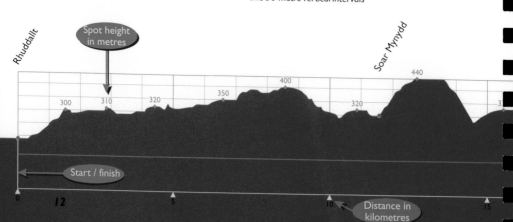

12

Transporting your bike

There are three ways of getting you and your bike to the start of a ride:

- **Cycle** to the start or to a point along a route
- **Take the train.** Always check in advance that you can take the bike on the train. Some trains allow only up to two bikes and you may need to make a reservation and pay a flat fee however long the journey. Always label your bike showing your name and destination station.
- **By motor vehicle.** You can carry the bikes:

Inside the vehicle. Many bikes have quick-release mechanisms on both wheels and the seatpost, which allow a quick dismantling of the bike to fit in even quite small cars.

On top of the vehicle. The advantages of this method are that the bikes are completely out of the way and are not resting against each other, you can get at the boot or hatch easily and the bikes do not obscure the number plate or rear lights and indicators.

On a rack that attaches to the rear of the vehicle. The advantages are that the rack and bikes are easily accessible, also fuel consumption is better than with a roof-rack.

Code of Conduct

- Enjoy the countryside and respect its life and work
- Only ride where you know you have a legal right
- Always yield to horses and pedestrians
- Take all litter with you
- Don't get annoyed with anyone; it never solves any problems
- Guard against all risk of fire
- Fasten all gates
- Keep your dogs under close control
- Keep to public paths across farmland
- Use gates and stiles to cross fences, hedges and walls
- Avoid livestock, crops and machinery or, if not possible, keep contact to a minimum
- Help keep all water clean
- Protect wildlife, plants and trees
- Take special care on country roads
- Make no unnecessary noise

Whichever way you carry the bikes on the outside of the vehicle, ensure that you regularly check that they are secure and that straps and fixings that hold them in place have not come loose. If you are leaving the bikes for any length of time, be sure they are secure against theft; if nothing else lock them to each other.

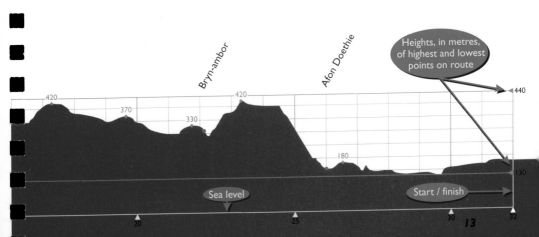

Legend to 1:50 000 maps

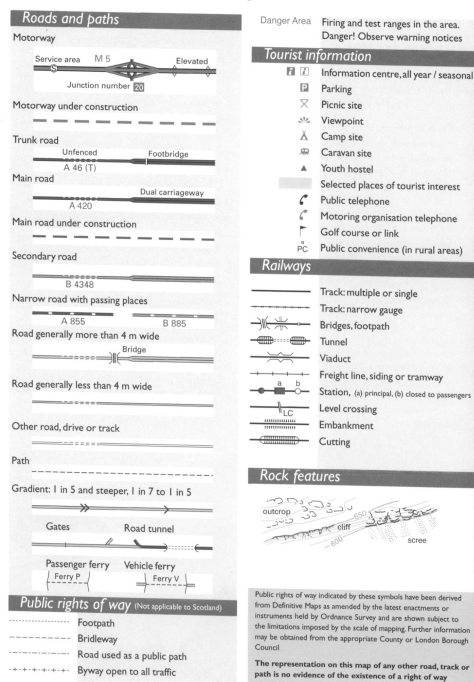

Roads and paths

Motorway

Service area   M 5   Elevated

Junction number 20

Motorway under construction

Trunk road

Unfenced   Footbridge
A 46 (T)

Main road

Dual carriageway
A 420

Main road under construction

Secondary road

B 4348

Narrow road with passing places

A 855   B 885

Road generally more than 4 m wide

Bridge

Road generally less than 4 m wide

Other road, drive or track

Path

Gradient: 1 in 5 and steeper, 1 in 7 to 1 in 5

Gates   Road tunnel

Passenger ferry   Vehicle ferry
Ferry P   Ferry V

Public rights of way (Not applicable to Scotland)

.... Footpath
— — — — — Bridleway
— · — · — · — Road used as a public path
-+-+-+-+-+-+- Byway open to all traffic

Danger Area   Firing and test ranges in the area. Danger! Observe warning notices

Tourist information

𝐢	𝑖	Information centre, all year / seasonal
P		Parking
✕		Picnic site
⚊		Viewpoint
Ⲭ		Camp site
⊞		Caravan site
▲		Youth hostel
		Selected places of tourist interest
ℭ		Public telephone
ℭ		Motoring organisation telephone
⌐		Golf course or link
PC		Public convenience (in rural areas)

Railways

— Track: multiple or single
Track: narrow gauge
Bridges, footpath
Tunnel
Viaduct
Freight line, siding or tramway
a   b
Station, (a) principal, (b) closed to passengers
LC   Level crossing
Embankment
Cutting

Rock features

outcrop   650
cliff
600   scree

Public rights of way indicated by these symbols have been derived from Definitive Maps as amended by the latest enactments or instruments held by Ordnance Survey and are shown subject to the limitations imposed by the scale of mapping. Further information may be obtained from the appropriate County or London Borough Council

The representation on this map of any other road, track or path is no evidence of the existence of a right of way

14

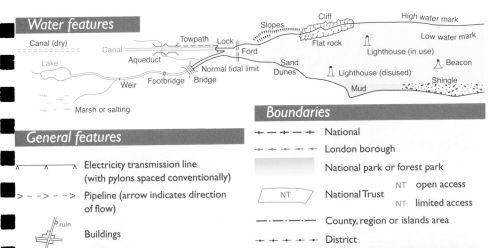

Water features

Canal (dry)
Canal
Aqueduct
Lake
Weir
Footbridge
Bridge
Marsh or salting
Towpath
Lock
Ford
Normal tidal limit
Slopes
Cliff
Flat rock
Sand Dunes
Mud
High water mark
Low water mark
Lighthouse (in use)
Lighthouse (disused)
Beacon
Shingle

General features

⋀ ⋀ ⋀	Electricity transmission line (with pylons spaced conventionally)
> - -> - ->	Pipeline (arrow indicates direction of flow)
ruin	Buildings
	Public buildings (selected)
⬭	Bus or coach station
	Coniferous wood
	Non-coniferous wood
	Mixed wood
	Orchard
	Park or ornamental grounds
	Quarry
	Spoil heap, refuse tip or dump
Ĭ	Radio or TV mast
♦	Church or chapel with tower
♦	Church or chapel with spire
+	Church or chapel without tower or spire
○	Chimney or tower
⌀	Glasshouse
┼	Graticule intersection at 5' intervals
Ⓗ	Heliport
△	Triangulation pillar
X	Windmill with or without sails
Ï	Windpump

Boundaries

+ — + — +	National
-◦- -◦- -◦-	London borough
	National park or forest park
NT	National Trust
	NT open access
	NT limited access
-·—·—·—	County, region or islands area
+ + + +	District

Abbreviations

P	Post office
PH	Public house
MS	Milestone
MP	Milepost
CH	Clubhouse
PC	Public convenience (in rural areas)
TH	Town hall, guildhall or equivalent
CG	Coastguard

Antiquities

VILLA	Roman
Castle	Non-Roman
⚔	Battlefield (with date)
☆	Tumulus
+	Position of antiquity which cannot be drawn to scale
𝔐	Ancient monuments and historic buildings in the care of the Secretaries of State for the Environment, for Scotland and for Wales and that are open to the public

Heights

—50—	Contours are at 10 metres vertical interval
·144	Heights are to the nearest metre above mean sea level

Heights shown close to a triangulation pillar refer to the station height at ground level and not necessarily to the summit

Across northwest Norfolk from Sandringham to Burnham Market

Start

The church in Dersingham, 14 km (9 miles) north of King's Lynn

P Car park near the church

Distance and grade

55 km (34 miles)

Easy

Terrain

Gently rolling arable land. Mixture of sandstone and flint houses. Lowest point – 7m (23 feet) just west of Burnham Market. Highest point – 80 m (262 feet) at North Pole Farm near Houghton Park (6)

Nearest Railway

King's Lynn, 13km (8 miles) south of the route at Sandringham

In the gently rolling land of the northwest corner of Norfolk through which this ride takes you, there is a division in the materials used for the construction of the older dwellings. To the west there is a high incidence of the dark yellow sandstone known as Norfolk Ragstone, used even when the individual stones are very small. Further east the old buildings are almost exclusively red-brick, flint or a combination of both. The ride starts by heading east away from the royal residence of Sandringham between attractive lines of beech and copper beech trees. The route turns north by Houghton Hall towards Burnham Market – an attractive village with interesting craft and antique shops. A quiet lane heads east to Ringstead where there is a tearoom at the Post Office and an excellent pub. South of Ringstead you may wish to make a diversion to visit the lavender fields at Heacham. Otherwise the route avoids the busy A149 by following quiet lanes through Sedgeford and Ingoldisthorpe to return to Dersingham.

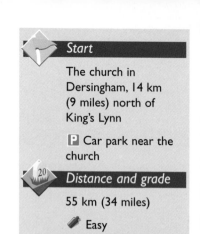

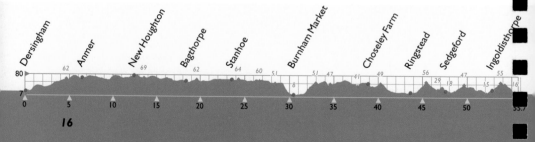

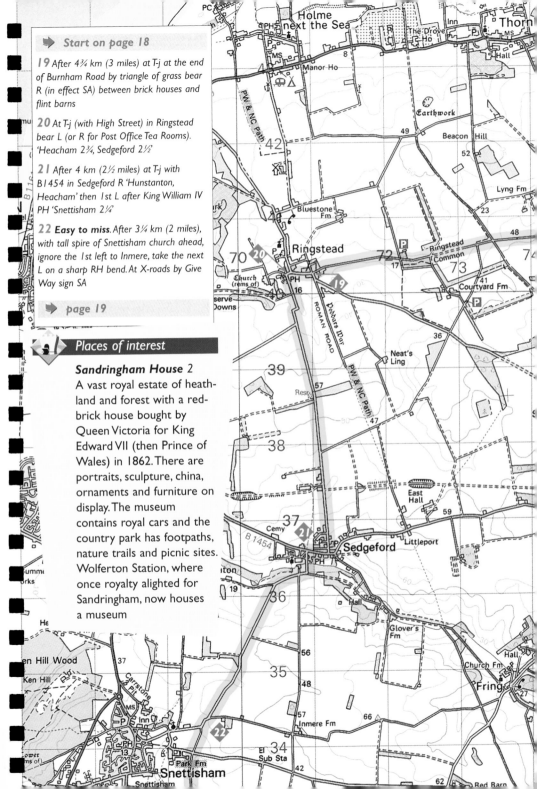

➡ **Start on page 18**

19 *After 4¾ km (3 miles) at T-j at the end of Burnham Road by triangle of grass bear R (in effect SA) between brick houses and flint barns*

20 *At T-j (with High Street) in Ringstead bear L (or R for Post Office Tea Rooms). 'Heacham 2¾, Sedgeford 2½'*

21 *After 4 km (2½ miles) at T-j with B1454 in Sedgeford R 'Hunstanton, Heacham' then 1st L after King William IV PH 'Snettisham 2¼'*

22 **Easy to miss**. *After 3¼ km (2 miles), with tall spire of Snettisham church ahead, ignore the 1st left to Inmere, take the next L on a sharp RH bend. At X-roads by Give Way sign SA*

➡ **page 19**

Places of interest

Sandringham House 2

A vast royal estate of heathland and forest with a redbrick house bought by Queen Victoria for King Edward VII (then Prince of Wales) in 1862. There are portraits, sculpture, china, ornaments and furniture on display. The museum contains royal cars and the country park has footpaths, nature trails and picnic sites. Wolferton Station, where once royalty alighted for Sandringham, now houses a museum

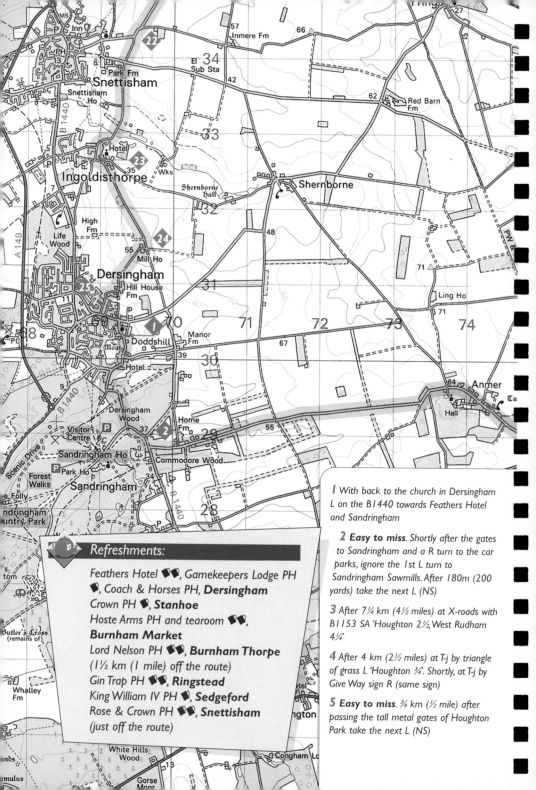

Refreshments:

Feathers Hotel 🍴🍴, Gamekeepers Lodge PH 🍴, Coach & Horses PH, **Dersingham**

Crown PH 🍴, **Stanhoe**

Hoste Arms PH and tearoom 🍴🍴, **Burnham Market**

Lord Nelson PH 🍴🍴, **Burnham Thorpe** (1½ km (1 mile) off the route)

Gin Trap PH 🍴🍴, **Ringstead**

King William IV PH 🍴, **Sedgeford**

Rose & Crown PH 🍴🍴, **Snettisham** (just off the route)

1 With back to the church in Dersingham L on the B1440 towards Feathers Hotel and Sandringham

2 Easy to miss. Shortly after the gates to Sandringham and a R turn to the car parks, ignore the 1st L turn to Sandringham Sawmills. After 180m (200 yards) take the next L (NS)

3 After 7¼ km (4½ miles) at X-roads with B1153 SA 'Houghton 2½, West Rudham 4¼'

4 After 4 km (2½ miles) at T-j by triangle of grass L 'Houghton ¾'. Shortly, at T-j by Give Way sign R (same sign)

5 Easy to miss. ¾ km (½ mile) after passing the tall metal gates of Houghton Park take the next L (NS)

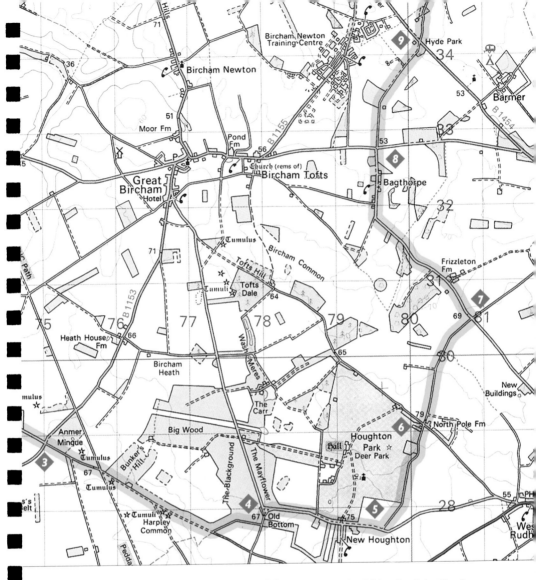

6 At X-roads by the brick and flint barns of North Pole Farm SA (NS)

7 At X-roads by Give Way sign and triangle of grass L (NS)

8 At X-roads by triangle of grass shortly after small flint church in Bagthorpe SA (NS)

9 At X-roads (with busy B1454) SA 'Barwick 1'

➡ **page 20**

22 **Easy to miss**. After 3¼ km (2 miles), with tall spire of Snettisham church ahead, ignore the 1st L to Inmere, take the next L on a sharp RH bend. At X-roads by Give Way sign SA

23 At T-j with Shernborne Road L

24 **Easy to miss**. After 1½ km (1 miles), shortly after brow of hill 1st R by triangle of grass and houses with neat hedges

25 At T-j in Dersingham at the bottom of the hill L (NS) and follow the road back to the start

10 At T-j (with B1155) by Give Way sign R. At T-j with Burnham Road by the pond in Stanhoe R 'Wells 10, Burnham Market 4'

11 1¼ km (¾ mile) after the Crown PH in Stanhoe next R 'North Creake 2'

12 After 1½ km (1 mile) 1st L at X-roads in the middle of brick and flint farm buildings 'Burnham Market'. Sea views

13 At T-j (with B1355) at the end of Beacon Hill Road L. At T-j with Front Street by the Lord Nelson PH L '6ft 6ins width limit'

14 At T-j by the memorial cross in the centre of Burnham Market turn L towards the church

15 Towards the end of the village 1st R 'Brancaster 2' then immediately L onto Ringstead Road

16 After 4¾ km (3 miles) at X-roads by Give Way sign SA (NS)

17 At X-roads with B1153 SA 'Ringstead 4'

18 At T-j by Give Way sign with Xmas Cottage ahead R then 1st L

← page 17

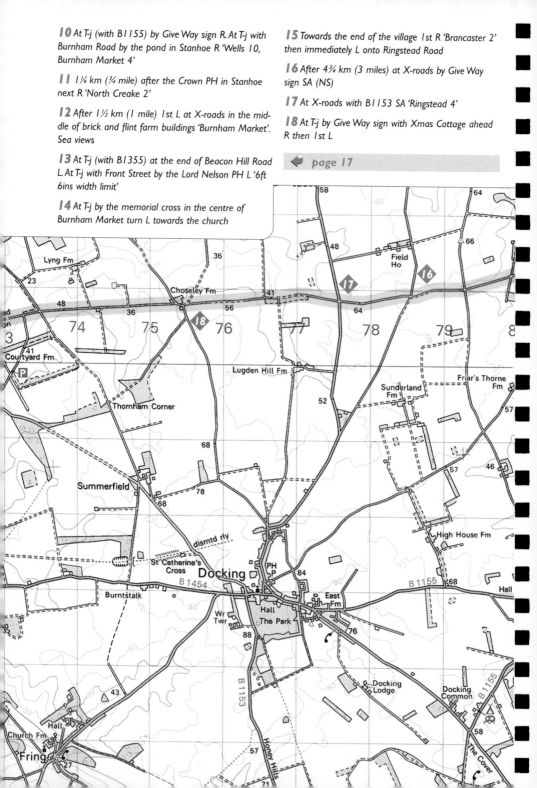

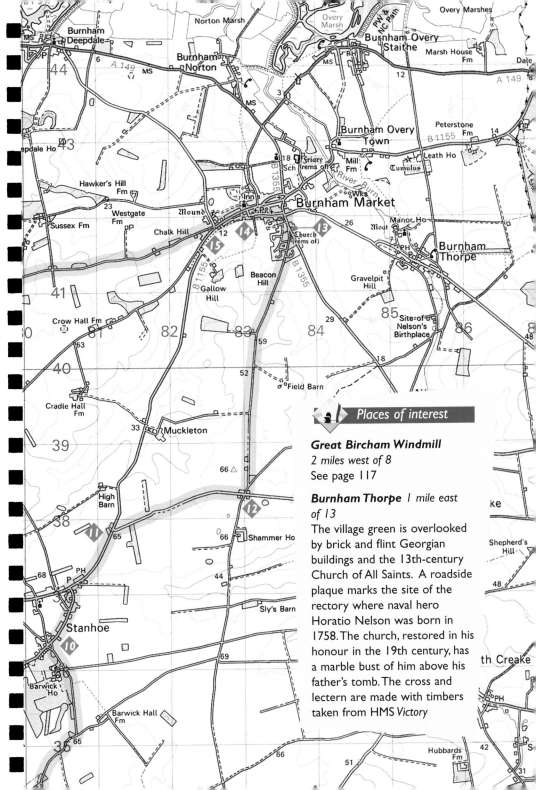

Places of interest

Great Bircham Windmill
2 miles west of 8
See page 117

Burnham Thorpe *1 mile east of 13*

The village green is overlooked by brick and flint Georgian buildings and the 13th-century Church of All Saints. A roadside plaque marks the site of the rectory where naval hero Horatio Nelson was born in 1758. The church, restored in his honour in the 19th century, has a marble bust of him above his father's tomb. The cross and lectern are made with timbers taken from HMS *Victory*

2 North from Fakenham to the coast at Wells-next-the-Sea

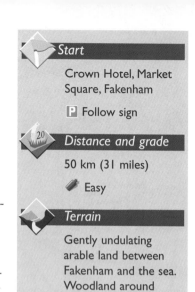

Start

Crown Hotel, Market Square, Fakenham

P Follow sign

Distance and grade

50 km (31 miles)

🥖 Easy

Terrain

Gently undulating arable land between Fakenham and the sea. Woodland around Holkham Park. Lowest point – sea level in Wells. Highest point – 66 m (220 feet) to the east of North Creake

Nearest railway

Sheringham, 25 km (15½ miles) east of Warham

One of three from Fakenham, this ride heads west then north to the coast at Wells-next-the-Sea, returning via Little Walsingham and Great Snoring. The ride starts by following the valley of the River Wensum, one of the four main rivers draining the east of Norfolk, all linking at Great Yarmouth. You pass fine round-towered flint churches in Shereford and Syderstone as you cross a gently rolling arable landscape, passing copses of broadleaf woodland, particularly in the stream and river valleys. A short, unavoidable section of busy road (the B1355) links the attractive flint villages of South and North Creake before the ride turns northeast, climbing to its highpoint at 66 m (220 ft) with fine views of the triumphal arch of Holkham Hall. A long, gentle, wooded descent leads down into Wells and a bustling waterfront. If you had coffee in North Creake and lunch in Wells, then it only remains to take tea in Little Walsingham, a charming village with a distinctly religious feel boasting a priory, an abbey and a shrine dedicated to the Virgin Mary.

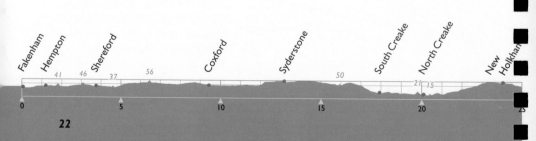

The three Fakenham rides could be linked up to form a 120-km (75-mile) circuit: start with Ride 4 (Fakenham to Castle Acre), leave it at instruction 23, join this ride (Fakenham to Wells) from instructions 8-20 then join Ride 3 (Fakenham – Blakeney) for instructions 11-32, following it back to the start.

Places of interest

South Creake 12
The village has one of East Anglia's finest churches, dating mainly from the 13th and 14th centuries. The medieval hammerbeam roof is decorated with carved angels. An unusual brass depicts a priest lying between his parents. The nave, 15th-century rood screen and pulpit are all magnificent

North Creake 13
Changing styles are reflected in St Mary's Church, founded in 1300, with the faded 'Doom' painting over the chancel arch, the Royal Arms of Charles I above the north door and a tasteful 1978 memorial chapel. Fragments of the old abbey remain – it had to close when the resident canons died in the 1504 plague

Refreshments:

Lots of choice in **Fakenham**
Lynn Arms PH, **Syderstone**
Jolly Farmers PH 🍴, tearoom, **North Creake**
Crown PH 🍴🍴, Ark Royal PH 🍴, Lifeboat PH 🍴, lots of choice in **Wells**
Three Horseshoes PH 🍴🍴, **Warham**
The Bull PH 🍴, Robin Hood Inn, **Walsingham**

▲ *Wells-next-the-Sea*

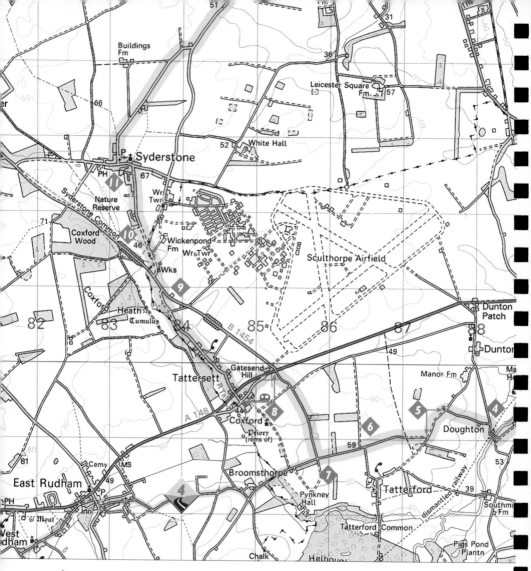

1 With back to the Crown Hotel in the Market Square, Fakenham, R onto Bridge Street 'Dereham B1146, Swaffham (A1065)

2 Cross the river. At X-roads (your priority) shortly after the end of the houses in Hempton turn R 'King's Lynn, Cromer A148'. At offset X-roads with A1065 SA 'Dunton 4, Shereford 2'

3 Through Shereford. ¾ km (½ mile) after the round flint church tower 1st R 'Dunton, Tatterford 1½'

4 Cross bridge over river then take the 1st L 'Tatterford'

5 At T-j L (NS) then after ¾ km (½ mile) 1st R 'Tattersett'

6 At T-j bear R (in effect SA) 'Broomsthorpe, Tattersett'

7 Follow road round to the R and signs for Tattersett

8 At X-roads with the A148 L then 1st L opposite garage. After ½ km (¼ mile) 1st R then at X-roads with A148 SA 'Tattersett'

9 At T-j with B1454 L 'Docking 6, Heacham 11' then 1st R 'Syderstone'

10 After ¾ km (½ mile) 1st L 'Syderstone ¾'

11 At T-j by the church in Syderstone L then 1st R 'South Creake 3'

➡ page 26

26 At 1st X-roads in Great Snoring (your priority) SA 'Fakenham'. At 2nd X-roads (also your priority) by telephone box and Great Snoring village sign R 'Unsuitable for HGVs'

27 After 4¾ km (3 miles) at roundabout with A148 3rd exit 'King's Lynn' (**take care** – busy road) then after 18m (20 yards) leave main road and bear

diagonally L onto narrow tarmac path. After 180m (200 yards) 1st L

28 At X-roads at the end of Thorpland Road SA onto Holt Road 'Fakenham Town Centre'

29 At T-j in the centre of Fakenham R onto Norwich Street (one way street) to return to the Market Square

12 After 4¾ km (3 miles) at T-j with B1355 in South Creake L 'Burnham Market 4'

13 Busy 2½ km (1½ miles) section. Go past church in North Creake and take the second R by telephone box onto Wells Road

14 Steady climb over 3¼ km (2 miles). At X-roads at the top of hill (arch to the left) L 'Wells 3½'

15 After 4 km (2½ miles) at T-j with B1105 L 'Wells'

16 After 2 km (1¼ miles) **ignore** 1st right to Hunstanton (A149). After further ½ km (¼ mile) take the next R 'Beach, Town Centre' then immediately L 'Beach, Car Park'

17 At T-j (with B1105) turn R along seafront and follow road round to the R

18 At T-j with Warham Road (A149) L 'Cromer' then R 'Warham, Wighton'

19 After 2½ km (1½ miles) 1st L 'Warham ½'

20 At X-roads by the Horseshoes PH in Warham R 'Wighton' [OR for link to Ride 3 Fakenham to Blakeney, SA past the Horseshoes PH and after 1½ km (1 miles) 1st L to join the other ride at instruction 11]

21 Lovely sunken lane, high hedgerows. At T-j by a triangle of grass and Give Way sign L then 1st R 'Walsingham'

22 At T-j (with B1388) R then R again by the telephone box 'Unbridged ford'. 1st L by memorial stone

23 At X-roads at the end of St Peters Road L. At T-j with a high flint wall ahead R 'Parking'

24 At T-j by brick lock-up at the end of square L then after 360 m (400 yards) 1st L onto Church Street

25 Go past church. At X-roads by Give Way sign R 'Great Snoring, Thursford'

26 At 1st X-roads in Great Snoring (your priority) SA 'Fakenham'. At 2nd X-roads (also your priority) by telephone box and Great Snoring village sign R 'Unsuitable for HGVs'

◀ page 25

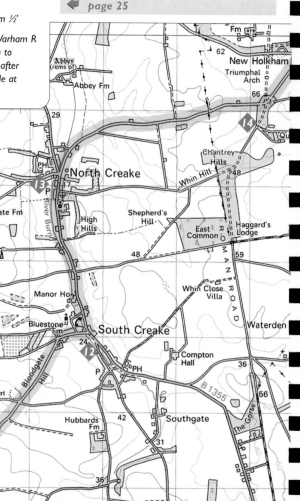

Northeast from Fakenham to the coast at Blakeney and Cley

The start of this ride follows the same course as the end of on-road route 2 which also links Fakenham with the coast. Both pass through the curiously named village of Great Snoring and the attractions of Little Walsingham with its abbey, priory and pretty flint houses. At Wighton, the routes diverge: this one now turns northeast towards the coast at Stiffkey ('Stooky') Blakeney and Cley ('Cly'), all bird-watching sites *par excellence*. The ride turns south, following the wooded valley of the River Glaven to Hunworth before entering the maze of tiny farm lanes south of Briston. Just 3 miles west of Briston is the one point in Norfolk where the land rises above the 100 metre contour line, near the junction of the B1354 and B1110.

Start

The Crown Hotel,
Market Square,
Fakenham

P Follow signs

Distance and grade

66 km (41 miles)

🖊 Easy

Terrain

Gently undulating arable land. Broadleaf copses. Coastline at Blakeney and Cley. Lowest point – sea level at Blakeney and Cley. Highest point – 77 m (253 ft) just west of Stibbard (30)

Refreshments

Lots of choice in **Fakenham**
Bull Inn 🍴, Robin Hood Inn, **Little Walsingham**
Red Lion PH 🍴🍴, **Stiffkey** *(just north of the route at 12)*
Bluebell PH, **Langham**
Kings Arms PH 🍴🍴, White Horse PH 🍴🍴,
lots of choice in **Blakeney**
George & Dragon PH 🍴, Three Swallows PH 🍴🍴,
Cley next the Sea
Kings Head PH 🍴, **Letheringsett**
Hunny Bell PH 🍴🍴, **Hunworth**
John Stracey PH 🍴, **Briston**
Boar Inn 🍴, **Great Ryburgh**

Nearest railway

Sheringham, 11km
(6¾ miles) east of Cley
next the Sea

Links

The three Fakenham
rides could be linked up
to form a 120-km
(75-mile) circuit (see
page 23).

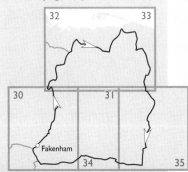

Fakenham

Places of interest

Fakenham 1

This attractive market town dates from
Saxon times and was a Royal Manor until
the 17th century. Its Market Place has
two old coaching inns both showing
traces of earlier work behind Georgian
façades, and the parish church has a
commanding 15th-century tower

Little Walsingham 24

A village with tall timbered houses lying
in a woodland setting. It was a medieval
place of pilgrimage noted for the Shrine
of Virgin Mary, founded in the 11th
century. The Augustinian friary and the
Franciscan Priory were added later. The
priory ruins are approached by a 15th-
century gateway in the High Street

▼ Cley next the Sea

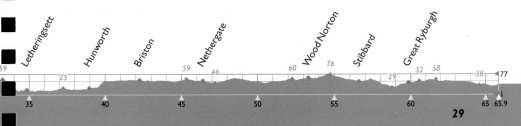

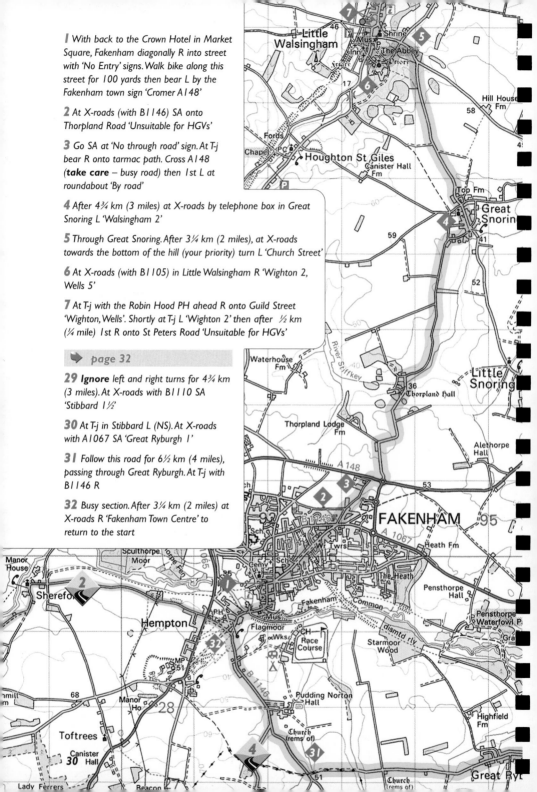

1 With back to the Crown Hotel in Market Square, Fakenham diagonally R into street with 'No Entry' signs. Walk bike along this street for 100 yards then bear L by the Fakenham town sign 'Cromer A148'

2 At X-roads (with B1146) SA onto Thorpland Road 'Unsuitable for HGVs'

3 Go SA at 'No through road' sign. At T-j bear R onto tarmac path. Cross A148 (**take care** – busy road) then 1st L at roundabout 'By road'

4 After 4¾ km (3 miles) at X-roads by telephone box in Great Snoring L 'Walsingham 2'

5 Through Great Snoring. After 3¼ km (2 miles), at X-roads towards the bottom of the hill (your priority) turn L 'Church Street'

6 At X-roads (with B1105) in Little Walsingham R 'Wighton 2, Wells 5'

7 At T-j with the Robin Hood PH ahead R onto Guild Street 'Wighton, Wells'. Shortly at T-j L 'Wighton 2' then after ½ km (¼ mile) 1st R onto St Peters Road 'Unsuitable for HGVs'

➡ **page 32**

29 **Ignore** left and right turns for 4¾ km (3 miles). At X-roads with B1110 SA 'Stibbard 1½'

30 At T-j in Stibbard L (NS). At X-roads with A1067 SA 'Great Ryburgh 1'

31 Follow this road for 6½ km (4 miles), passing through Great Ryburgh. At T-j with B1146 R

32 Busy section. After 3¼ km (2 miles) at X-roads R 'Fakenham Town Centre' to return to the start

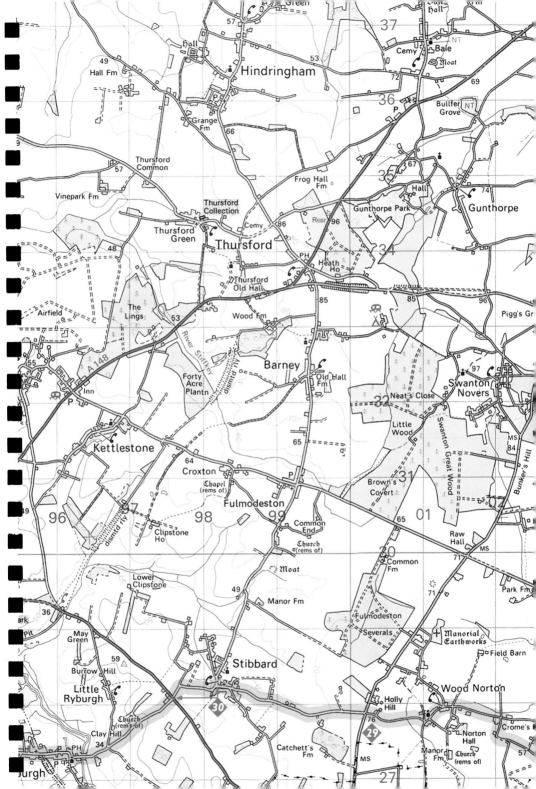

8 At T-j by memorial cross and triangle of grass bear R (in effect SA). At T-j by telephone box L 'Binham 3' then 1st L (NS)

9 After 2½ km (1½ miles) 1st R in Wighton. At X-roads SA 'Binham, Holt' then at T-j R

10 After 1¼ km (¾ mile) 1st L by Nutwood Farm 'Warham 2, Stiffkey 2½'

11 At X-roads SA 'Stiffkey'

12 At T-j (sea views) L to visit Stiffkey or R for continuation of route 'Cockthorpe 1, Binham 2, Langham 2½'

13 After 4 km (2½ miles) at T-j (with B1388) L 'Blakeney 2½'. Shortly after the Bluebell PH 1st L 'Blakeney B1388'

14 At X-roads with A149 SA onto Westgate Street 'Blakeney Quay' then 1st R after Blakeney Hotel onto High Street

15 At the end of High Street, at X-roads with A149 L 'Cromer'

16 This 1½ km (1 miles) section may be busy. Use the pavement with discretion. After crossing river, on sharp LH bend follow main road to the L to visit Cley or turn R here for continuation of route 'Car Park. Church'

17 After 1¼ km (¾ mile), 1st R by Three Swallows PH 'Wiveton 1, Glandford 1½'

18 At X-roads SA 'Glandford'

19 After 5¾ km (3½ miles) at X-roads with A148 SA 'Water Mill' and follow road round to the R over bridge. At X-roads L 'Thornage 2, Melton Constable 4'

20 After 1¼ km (¾ mile) 1st L 'Hunworth, Briston'

➡ page 35

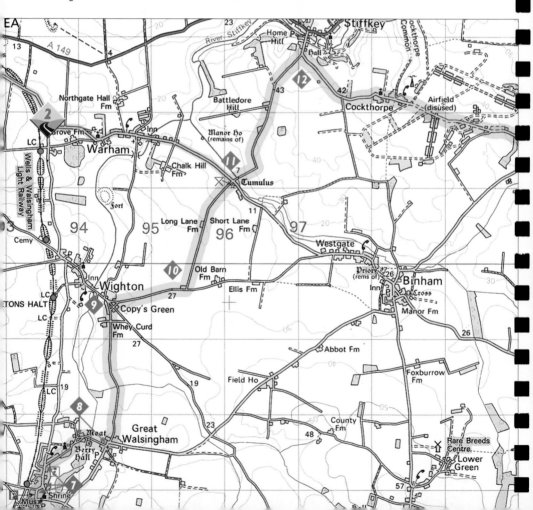

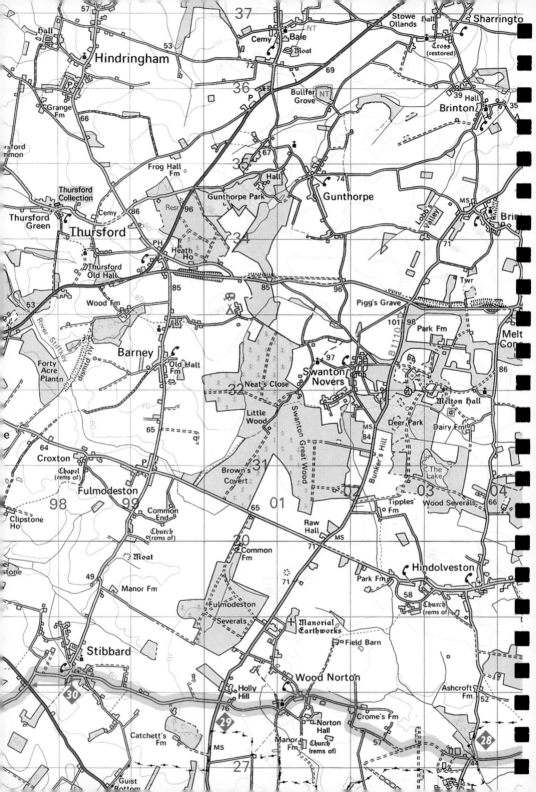

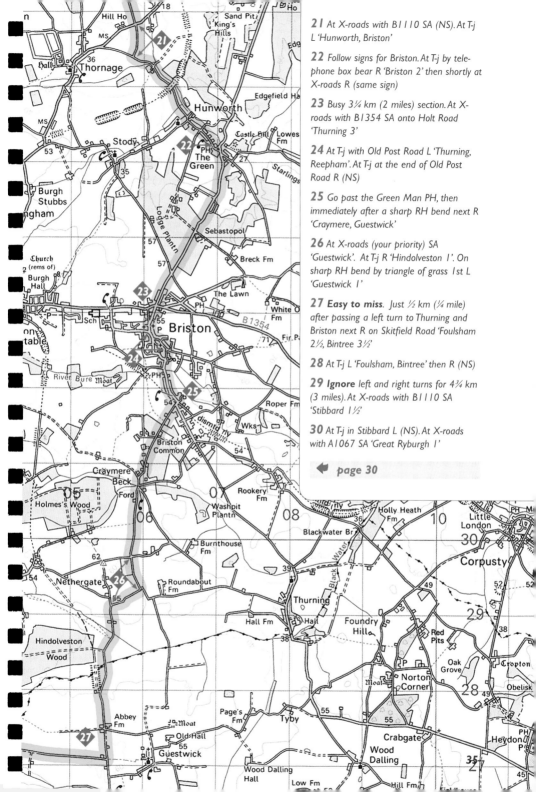

21 At X-roads with B1110 SA (NS). At T-j L 'Hunworth, Briston'

22 Follow signs for Briston. At T-j by telephone box bear R 'Briston 2' then shortly at X-roads R (same sign)

23 Busy 3¼ km (2 miles) section. At X-roads with B1354 SA onto Holt Road 'Thurning 3'

24 At T-j with Old Post Road L 'Thurning, Reepham'. At T-j at the end of Old Post Road R (NS)

25 Go past the Green Man PH, then immediately after a sharp RH bend next R 'Craymere, Guestwick'

26 At X-roads (your priority) SA 'Guestwick'. At T-j R 'Hindolveston 1'. On sharp RH bend by triangle of grass 1st L 'Guestwick 1'

27 **Easy to miss.** Just ½ km (¼ mile) after passing a left turn to Thurning and Briston next R on Skitfield Road 'Foulsham 2½, Bintree 3½'

28 At T-j L 'Foulsham, Bintree' then R (NS)

29 **Ignore** left and right turns for 4¾ km (3 miles). At X-roads with B1110 SA 'Stibbard 1½'

30 At T-j in Stibbard L (NS). At X-roads with A1067 SA 'Great Ryburgh 1'

◀ **page 30**

4 Southwest from Fakenham to Castle Acre

Castle Acre is one of the most attractive villages in Norfolk: it not only makes a good base for a few days exploring the lanes and tracks in the area, but is also a fine stopping point to aim for half-way round a ride as it has plenty to see, notably the castle and the priory, and several refreshment stops. From Fakenham the ride leaves the valley of the River Wensum, which flows east to the coast at Yarmouth, and after passing through the attractive villages of Whissonsett and Litcham drops into the valley of the River Nar, which flows west into the Great Ouse and thence into The Wash near King's Lynn. After exploring the flint and red-brick delights of Castle Acre the ride turns north through Rougham, passing between hawthorn hedgerows and intensively cultivated fields to arrive at Great Massingham, with its five ponds and wide village green. Carefully avoiding the busy A148 the route threads its way through the Rudhams and Broomsthorpe, rejoins the valley of the River Wensum and passes the pretty round flint church tower in Shereford before returning to the old market square in the heart of Fakenham.

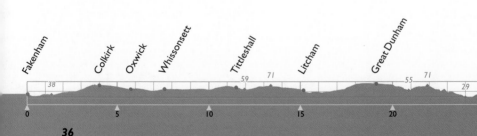

Links

The three Fakenham rides could be linked up to form a 120-km (75-mile) circuit (see page 23).

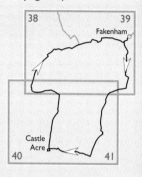

38 39
Fakenham

Castle
Acre
40 41

▶ Castle Acre Priory

Refreshments

Lots of choice in **Fakenham**
The Crown PH ●●, **Colkirk**
Swan Inn, **Whissonsett**
The Bull PH ●, **Litcham**
Ostrich PH ●●, *Albert Victor PH,*
tearooms, **Castle Acre**
Rose & Crown PH, **Great**
Massingham
Crown PH, Cat & Fiddle PH,
East Rudham

Places of interest

Castle Acre 9
The village is situated on the ancient Peddars Way and boasts a huge Norman castle mound and green, entered through a 13th century gate. The remains of the priory feature fine 12th-century arcading. There are painted panels in the 15th-century Church of St James

Rougham
Great Massingham
East Rudham
Shereford

70   86   68   64 82   43   37 46   41   87
                                                      28
30   35   40   45   50   54.7

1 With back to the Crown Hotel in the Market Square, Fakenham, R onto Bridge Street 'Dereham B1146, Swaffham (A1065)

2 Cross the river. At X-roads (your priority) shortly after the end of the houses in Hempton turn L 'Racecourse. East Dereham B1146'

3 After 1½ km (1 miles) 1st R 'Colkirk'

4 Follow the road through Colkirk. Shortly after the Crown PH 2nd L on Whissonsett Road 'Whissonsett'

5 After 4 km (2½ miles), at T-j by the Swan PH in Whissonsett R 'Raynhams 2½, Tittleshall 3'. Shortly, fork L onto Mill Lane

➥ **page 40**

17 After 3¼ km (2 miles), at X-roads in Great Massingham with a large pond to the right turn R 'Harpley 2¼'

18 Towards the end of the village, shortly after the no through road of Mill Lane to the right, next R on Rudham Road 'West Raynham 3¼'

19 After ¾ km (½ mile), with a red brick bungalow to the left, on a sharp RH bend bear L (in effect SA). At X-roads by the Gate House SA (NS). At next X-roads SA (NS)

20 After 3¼ km (2 miles) **ignore** 1st right by telephone box. Take the next R by a triangle of grass with a wooden bench (near to red-brick Hillside Cottages)

21 Shortly before T-j with main road (A148) in East Rudham turn R onto parallel lane with flint and brick wall / railings to your right. At T-j R then 1st L onto Broomsthorpe Road

22 After 2½ km (1½ miles) ignore 1st left. Shortly after passing a large brick and flint house to the left take the next L 'Tatterford 1¼'

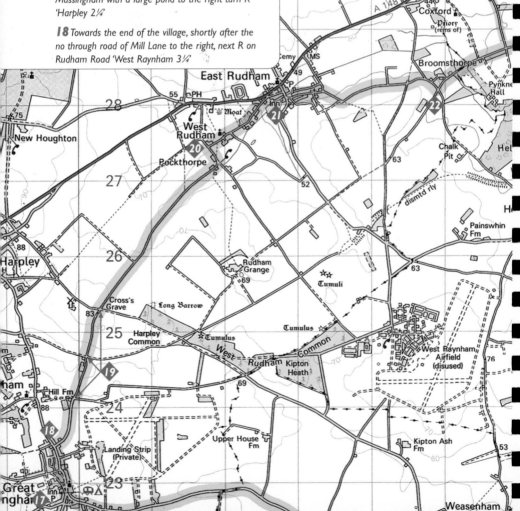

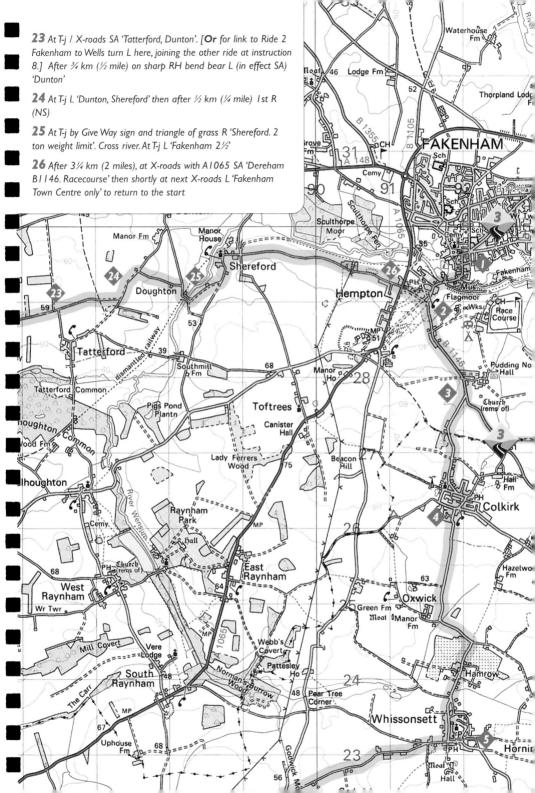

23 At T-j / X-roads SA 'Tatterford, Dunton'. [**Or** for link to Ride 2 Fakenham to Wells turn L here, joining the other ride at instruction 8.] After ¾ km (½ mile) on sharp RH bend bear L (in effect SA) 'Dunton'

24 At T-j L 'Dunton, Shereford' then after ½ km (¼ mile) 1st R (NS)

25 At T-j by Give Way sign and triangle of grass R 'Shereford. 2 ton weight limit'. Cross river. At T-j L 'Fakenham 2½'

26 After 3¼ km (2 miles), at X-roads with A1065 SA 'Dereham B1146. Racecourse' then shortly at next X-roads L 'Fakenham Town Centre only' to return to the start

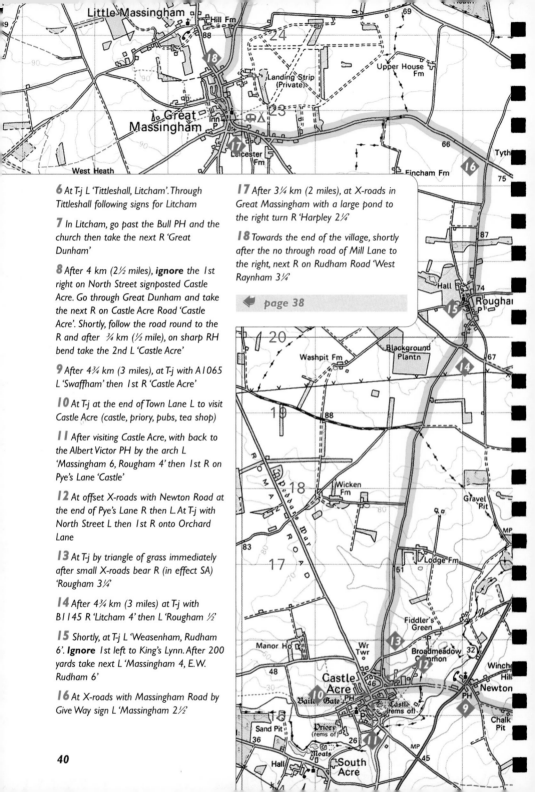

6 At T-j L 'Tittleshall, Litcham'. Through Tittleshall following signs for Litcham

7 In Litcham, go past the Bull PH and the church then take the next R 'Great Dunham'

8 After 4 km (2½ miles), **ignore** the 1st right on North Street signposted Castle Acre. Go through Great Dunham and take the next R on Castle Acre Road 'Castle Acre'. Shortly, follow the road round to the R and after ¾ km (½ mile), on sharp RH bend take the 2nd L 'Castle Acre'

9 After 4¾ km (3 miles), at T-j with A1065 L 'Swaffham' then 1st R 'Castle Acre'

10 At T-j at the end of Town Lane L to visit Castle Acre (castle, priory, pubs, tea shop)

11 After visiting Castle Acre, with back to the Albert Victor PH by the arch L 'Massingham 6, Rougham 4' then 1st R on Pye's Lane 'Castle'

12 At offset X-roads with Newton Road at the end of Pye's Lane R then L. At T-j with North Street L then 1st R onto Orchard Lane

13 At T-j by triangle of grass immediately after small X-roads bear R (in effect SA) 'Rougham 3¼'

14 After 4¾ km (3 miles) at T-j with B1145 R 'Litcham 4' then L 'Rougham ½'

15 Shortly, at T-j L 'Weasenham, Rudham 6'. **Ignore** 1st left to King's Lynn. After 200 yards take next L 'Massingham 4, E.W. Rudham 6'

16 At X-roads with Massingham Road by Give Way sign L 'Massingham 2½'

17 After 3¼ km (2 miles), at X-roads in Great Massingham with a large pond to the right turn R 'Harpley 2¼'

18 Towards the end of the village, shortly after the no through road of Mill Lane to the right, next R on Rudham Road 'West Raynham 3¼'

◀ **page 38**

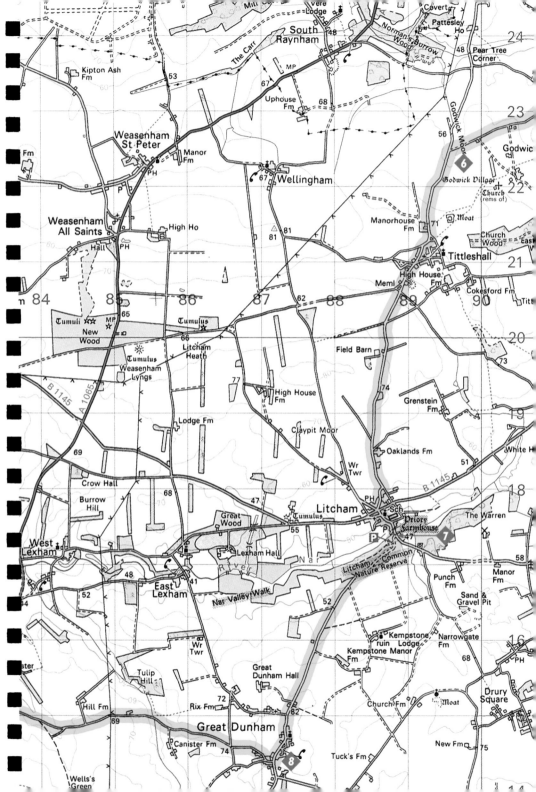

5 North from Aylsham to the coast at Cromer

Two on-road rides start from Aylsham as do the railway path rides known as Weavers' Way and Marriotts Way (see off-road rides 3 and 4). Aylsham is an attractive town with a fine square and is a good base for touring the northeast corner of Norfolk. This part of the region is less intensively cultivated than the land further to the west; there are more fields left to permanent pasture, more trees and woodland and even some common land at Abel Heath to the west of Aylsham, near the start of the ride. The overall impresion is nevertheless one of gently rolling arable land dotted with flint churches and occasional attractive old red-brick buildings. Flint is the preferred stone for most of the churches, including the round tower of the church at Bessingham, and sometimes for the bigger houses – note the fine decorated brick and flint window surrounds at Metton Hall and the imposing flint façade of Cromer Hall just to the south of the town. The ride makes its way north to the coast via a maze of quiet lanes then drops over 60 m (200 feet) in the last mile to reach Cromer before climbing up away from the coast to Northrepps and lanes back to Aylsham.

Start

The Post Office / Blackboys Inn, Aylsham, north of Norwich

P Follow signs

Distance and grade

55 km (34 miles)

Easy

Terrain

Undulating arable land, occasional broadleaf woodland, coast. Lowest point – sea level at Cromer. Highest point – 74 m (243 feet) southeast of Cromer

Nearest railway

Cromer

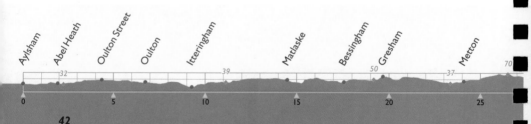

Places of interest

Blickling Hall *1 mile north of (3)*
A Jacobean 17th-century moated hall with an immaculate formal garden and impressive period-style rooms. A huge tapestry hanging in the Peter the Great Room depicts the Russian ruler, and the Long Gallery has an ornate plaster ceiling. There are extensive walks, a crescent-shaped lake, an orangery and a temple in the grounds

Mannington Hall Gardens *between 6 and 7*
Set around a moated 15th-century house and entered over a drawbridge, the gardens consist of extensive lawns enclosed by yew hedges with statuary busts. There are hundreds of different roses in the Heritage Rose Gardens, a lake with a stone bridge, woodland paths and nature trails

Refreshments:

Greens PH ☙, lots of choice in **Aylsham**
Walpole Arms PH ☙, **Itteringham**
Chequers PH, **Gresham**
Bath House PH ☙, Red Lion PH ☙, lots of choice in **Cromer**
Foundary Arms PH, **Northrepps**
Vernon Arms PH, **Southrepps**

Felbrigg Hall *1 mile off the route between 11 and 12*
Jacobean home of the Windham family for three centuries, built around 1620. There are furnishings and pictures from the 18th century, windows with medieval stained glass, elegant rococo plasterwork and a Gothic library. The grounds contain a walled garden, orangery, woodland and lakeside walks

Cromer *13–15*
Popular family resort with a sandy beach, the Pavilion Theatre and the Lifeboat Museum. The church tower is the tallest in Norfolk at 48 m (160 ft). A row of Victorian fishermen's cottages forms Cromer Museum, with crabbing industry displays

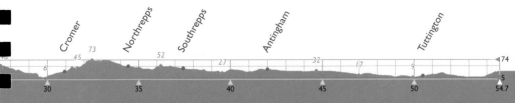

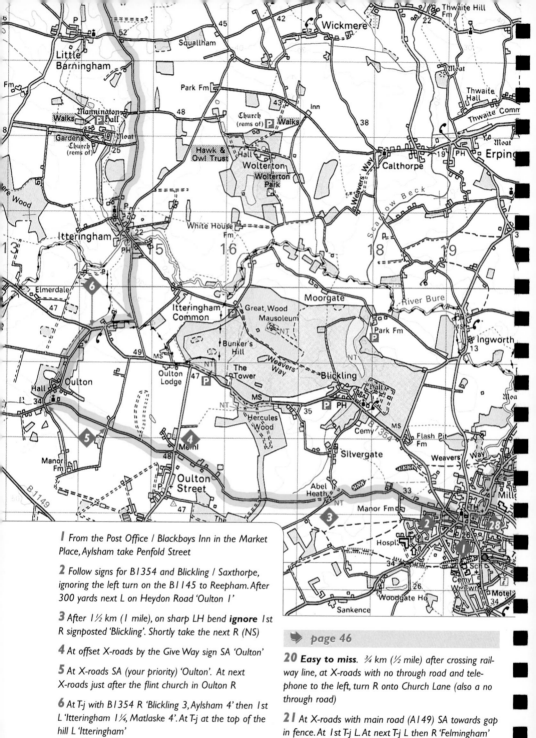

1 *From the Post Office / Blackboys Inn in the Market Place, Aylsham take Penfold Street*

2 *Follow signs for B1354 and Blickling / Saxthorpe, ignoring the left turn on the B1145 to Reepham. After 300 yards next L on Heydon Road 'Oulton 1'*

3 *After 1½ km (1 mile), on sharp LH bend **ignore** 1st R signposted 'Blickling'. Shortly take the next R (NS)*

4 *At offset X-roads by the Give Way sign SA 'Oulton'*

5 *At X-roads SA (your priority) 'Oulton'. At next X-roads just after the flint church in Oulton R*

6 *At T-j with B1354 R 'Blickling 3, Aylsham 4' then 1st L 'Itteringham 1¼, Matlaske 4'. At T-j at the top of the hill L 'Itteringham'*

➡ *page 46*

20 **Easy to miss**. *¾ km (½ mile) after crossing railway line, at X-roads with no through road and telephone to the left, turn R onto Church Lane (also a no through road)*

21 *At X-roads with main road (A149) SA towards gap in fence. At 1st T-j L. At next T-j L then R 'Felmingham'*

22 After 4 km (2½ miles) at T-j with B1145 bear R (in effect SA) ie do not turn right to Suffield, then shortly, on sharp RH bend 1st L 'Skeyton 1½, Coltishall 6'

23 Shortly after passing beneath railway bridge next R (NS)

24 At T-j by triangle of grass R 'Tuttington 1, Banningham 2' [**or** turn L 'Skeyton 1¼, Westwick 3' for link to on-road route 6 and follow signs for Scottow and Buxton]

25 At T-j with Norwich Road R 'Banningham' then L immediately after round-towered flint church

26 At X-roads with A140 SA towards wooden gate then lane

27 At T-j by round silos L. At T-j at the end of Dunkirk L 'Town Centre'

28 At T-j with Red Lion Street at the end of White Hart Street L 'Town Centre' then 1st R to return to the start

▲ Cromer

14 At next X-roads SA. At T-j with seafront R then 1st L on RH bend '6ft 6ins width limit'

15 At T-j with Church Street L then at traffic lights L onto B1159 'Mundesley'

16 Ignore right turn to hospital. 135 m (150 yards) after the brow of the hill take the 2nd R on Northrepps Road

17 Follow signs for Northrepps for 3¼ km (2 miles) ignoring right and left turns. Shortly after the Foundary Arms PH in Northrepps next R onto Craft Lane 'Southrepps 1½'

18 At T-j by the Vernon Arms PH in Southrepps R 'Thorpe Market 1¼, Roughton 2¾ then 1st L on Long Lane 'Gunton station'

19 At T-j at the end of Chapel Road R 'Railway Station'

← **page 44**

7 Follow this road for 6½ km (4 miles), passing through Itteringham and following signs for Matlaske. At X-roads by Give Way sign R 'Matlaske, Aldborough'

8 Through Matlaske past the round-towered church then after sharp RH and LH bend, climb through woodland and take the 1st L 'Bessingham ½, Sheringham 5½'

9 At T-j by church bear L uphill 'Gresham'

10 At X-roads by the round-towered church in Gresham R 'Metton 2¾, Cromer 5¼'

11 Follow signs for Metton through Gresham. ¾ km (½ mile) after the end of the village turn R by triangle of grass and memorial cross 'Metton 1½, Roughton 3½'

12 Follow this road for 5¾ km (3½ miles), passing through Metton. At X-roads (with B1436) by Give Way sign SA

13 After 3¼ km (2 miles) at X-roads at the end of Hall Road in Cromer SA onto Cabbell Road

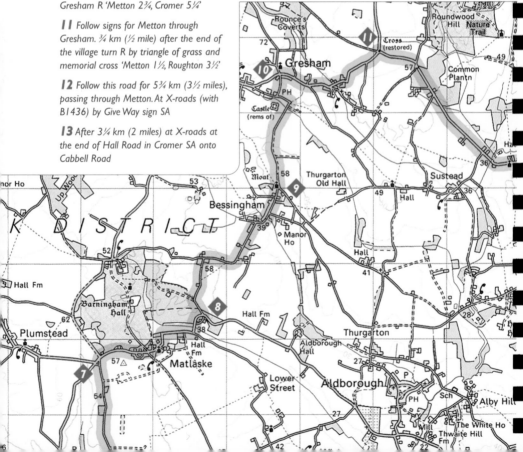

6 From Aylsham to Wroxham in the heart of the Norfolk Broads

Start

The Blackboys Inn, Aylsham, north of Norwich

P Follow signs

Distance and grade

56 kms (35 miles)

Easy

Terrain

Lowest point – sea level near the Broads. Highest point – 32 m (105 feet) at Skeyton (3)

Nearest railway

Hoveton

This second ride from the attractive town of Aylsham heads southeast towards the Broads and into Wroxham, the busy heart of the boating activity in the region. The land is predominantly arable with some pasture and clumps of broadleaf woodland, although the 'Oak Belt' to the south of Swanton Abbott is more pine than oak. The hedgerows are mainly hawthorn and it is heartening to see that in places more hedges have been planted, reversing a trend of many years which saw fields growing larger and larger with the consequent loss of hedgerows and the wildlife corridors that they provide. The ride passes large, old, thatched red-brick barns near to Sloley Hall on its way east into Broads country at Irstead. In the Broads one has the impression of more woodland, more thatched houses and a slightly more relaxed attitude towards land use. Of architectural note is a delightful thatched flint-and-brick house just south of Irstead and the thatched red-brick church of St Peters just north of Hoveton. Wroxham's role as boating centre can be seen in the flotillas of boats ready for hire at the bridge over the River Bure. It is a bustling town with the busy A1151 passing through it on its way towards Norwich. The course of the River Bure is followed roughly northwest from Wroxham back towards Aylsham, rejoining the outwards route near Burgh.

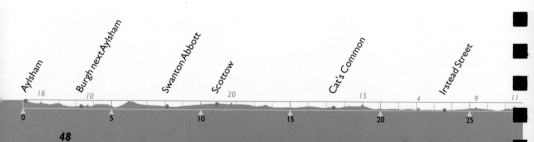

48

Links

It is possible to link this ride to Ride 9, which heads south from Wroxham to Reedham.

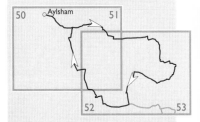

▼ Horning

Places of interest

Aylsham /
A market town with splendid old buildings: the Manor House and Abbots Hall date from the early 1600s and the Old Hall from 1689. The rose-covered grave of the landscape gardener Humphry Repton lies in the churchyard of the 14th-century St Michael's Church

Bure Valley Railway /
A narrow gauge line runs along the trackbed of the old Great Eastern for 15km (9 miles) beside the River Bure, between Aylsham and Wroxham

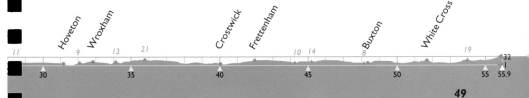

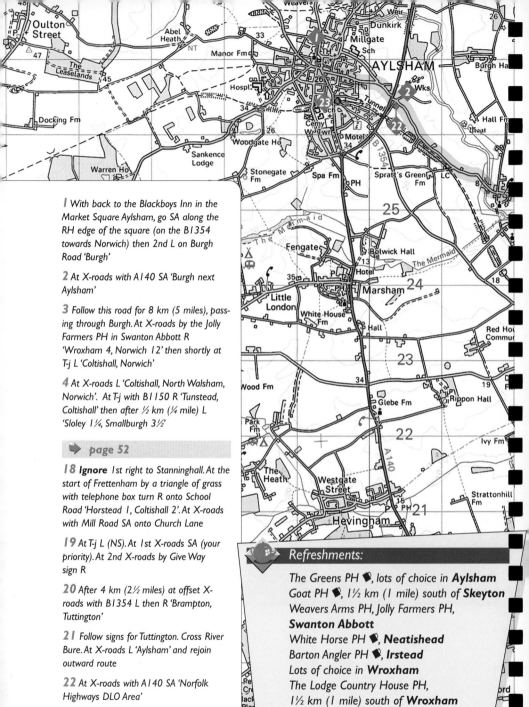

1 With back to the Blackboys Inn in the Market Square Aylsham, go SA along the RH edge of the square (on the B1354 towards Norwich) then 2nd L on Burgh Road 'Burgh'

2 At X-roads with A140 SA 'Burgh next Aylsham'

3 Follow this road for 8 km (5 miles), passing through Burgh. At X-roads by the Jolly Farmers PH in Swanton Abbott R 'Wroxham 4, Norwich 12' then shortly at T-j L 'Coltishall, Norwich'

4 At X-roads L 'Coltishall, North Walsham, Norwich'. At T-j with B1150 R 'Tunstead, Coltishall' then after ½ km (¼ mile) L 'Sloley 1¼, Smallburgh 3½'

➡ *page 52*

18 **Ignore** 1st right to Stanninghall. At the start of Frettenham by a triangle of grass with telephone box turn R onto School Road 'Horstead 1, Coltishall 2'. At X-roads with Mill Road SA onto Church Lane

19 At T-j L (NS). At 1st X-roads SA (your priority). At 2nd X-roads by Give Way sign R

20 After 4 km (2½ miles) at offset X-roads with B1354 L then R 'Brampton, Tuttington'

21 Follow signs for Tuttington. Cross River Bure. At X-roads L 'Aylsham' and rejoin outward route

22 At X-roads with A140 SA 'Norfolk Highways DLO Area'

23 At T-j in Aylsham R to return to the start

Refreshments:

The Greens PH 🍴, lots of choice in **Aylsham**
Goat PH 🍴, 1½ km (1 mile) south of **Skeyton**
Weavers Arms PH, Jolly Farmers PH, **Swanton Abbott**
White Horse PH 🍴, **Neatishead**
Barton Angler PH 🍴, **Irstead**
Lots of choice in **Wroxham**
The Lodge Country House PH, 1½ km (1 mile) south of **Wroxham**
Black Lion PH, **Buxton**

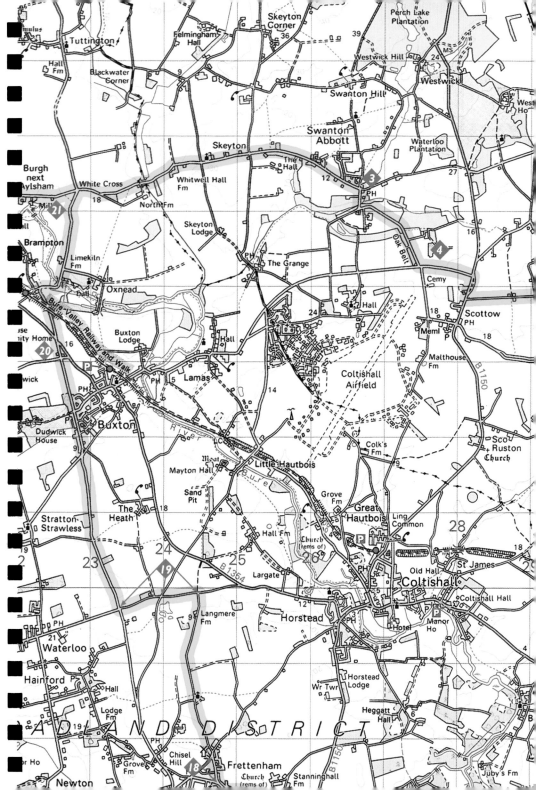

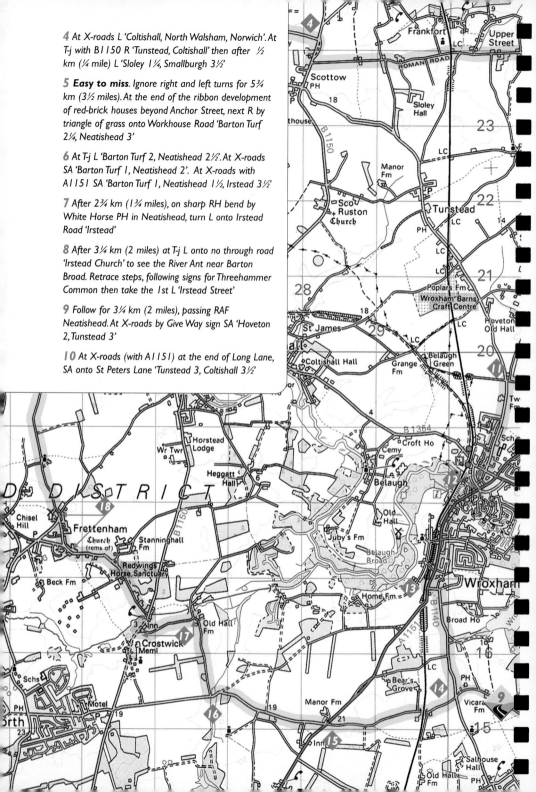

4 At X-roads L 'Coltishall, North Walsham, Norwich'. At T-j with B1150 R 'Tunstead, Coltishall' then after ½ km (¼ mile) L 'Sloley 1¼, Smallburgh 3½'

5 Easy to miss. Ignore right and left turns for 5¾ km (3½ miles). At the end of the ribbon development of red-brick houses beyond Anchor Street, next R by triangle of grass onto Workhouse Road 'Barton Turf 2¼, Neatishead 3'

6 At T-j L 'Barton Turf 2, Neatishead 2½'. At X-roads SA 'Barton Turf 1, Neatishead 2'. At X-roads with A1151 SA 'Barton Turf 1, Neatishead 1½, Irstead 3½'

7 After 2¾ km (1¾ miles), on sharp RH bend by White Horse PH in Neatishead, turn L onto Irstead Road 'Irstead'

8 After 3¼ km (2 miles) at T-j L onto no through road 'Irstead Church' to see the River Ant near Barton Broad. Retrace steps, following signs for Threehammer Common then take the 1st L 'Irstead Street'

9 Follow for 3¼ km (2 miles), passing RAF Neatishead. At X-roads by Give Way sign SA 'Hoveton 2, Tunstead 3'

10 At X-roads (with A1151) at the end of Long Lane, SA onto St Peters Lane 'Tunstead 3, Coltishall 3½'

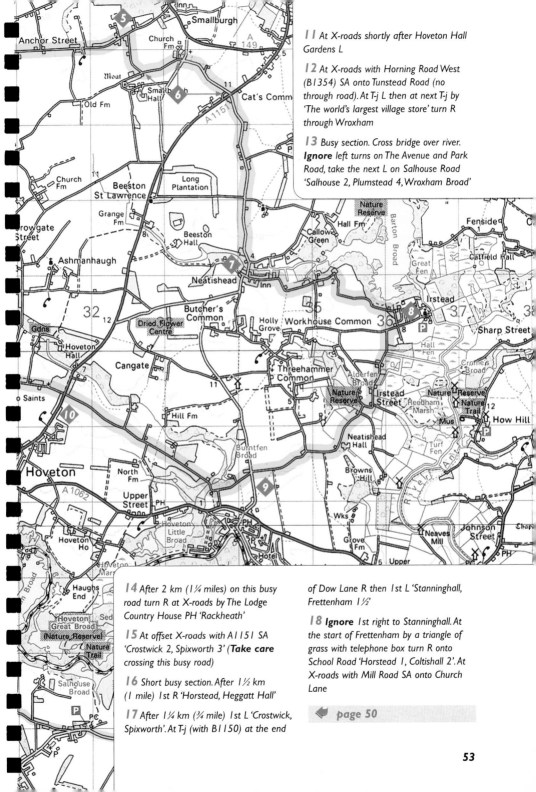

11 At X-roads shortly after Hoveton Hall Gardens L

12 At X-roads with Horning Road West (B1354) SA onto Tunstead Road (no through road). At T-j L then at next T-j by 'The world's largest village store' turn R through Wroxham

13 Busy section. Cross bridge over river. **Ignore** left turns on The Avenue and Park Road, take the next L on Salhouse Road 'Salhouse 2, Plumstead 4, Wroxham Broad'

14 After 2 km (1¼ miles) on this busy road turn R at X-roads by The Lodge Country House PH 'Rackheath'

15 At offset X-roads with A1151 SA 'Crostwick 2, Spixworth 3' (**Take care** crossing this busy road)

16 Short busy section. After 1½ km (1 mile) 1st R 'Horstead, Heggatt Hall'

17 After 1¼ km (¾ mile) 1st L 'Crostwick, Spixworth'. At T-j (with B1150) at the end

of Dow Lane R then 1st L 'Stanninghall, Frettenham 1½'

18 **Ignore** 1st right to Stanninghall. At the start of Frettenham by a triangle of grass with telephone box turn R onto School Road 'Horstead 1, Coltishall 2'. At X-roads with Mill Road SA onto Church Lane

◀ page 50

From Swaffham to Cockley Cley, the Nar Valley and Castle Acre

7

Swaffham has a fine, wide market square in its centre and many attractive old buildings stand around the edge of the square. The town lies on the geological divide between the chalk and flint to the north and the sandier soils of Breckland to the south. Towards Brandon and Thetford the land is good only for forestry plantations of pines, in complete contrast to the richer soils in the rest of East Anglia. The ride heads southwest to Cockley Cley where there is a fascinating recreation of an Iceni village; the Iceni were the tribe led by Queen Boudicca who gave their name to the Icknield Way which runs from the Thames near Goring to the start of the Peddars Way near Thetford. The twisted Scots Pines near to Cockley Cley were caused by the original hedges being allowed to grow up due to lack of manpower during World War I. Glimpses of Oxborough Hall can be caught through the iron gates at the western end of the village. The tall lime trees and the slightly decayed, untouched feel about the nature reserve near Oxborough Wood stand in dramatic contrast to the intensive land use all around.

Start

White Hart Inn, Market Square, Swaffham

P Follow signs

Distance and grade

55 kms (34 miles)

Easy

Terrain

Sandy woodland south of Swaffham, open, arable farmland, wooded valley of the River Nar. Lowest point – 3m (10 feet) at the Oxborough Wood Nature Reserve (5). Highest point – 85m (280 feet) between Newton and Sporle (15-16)

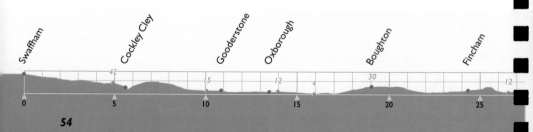

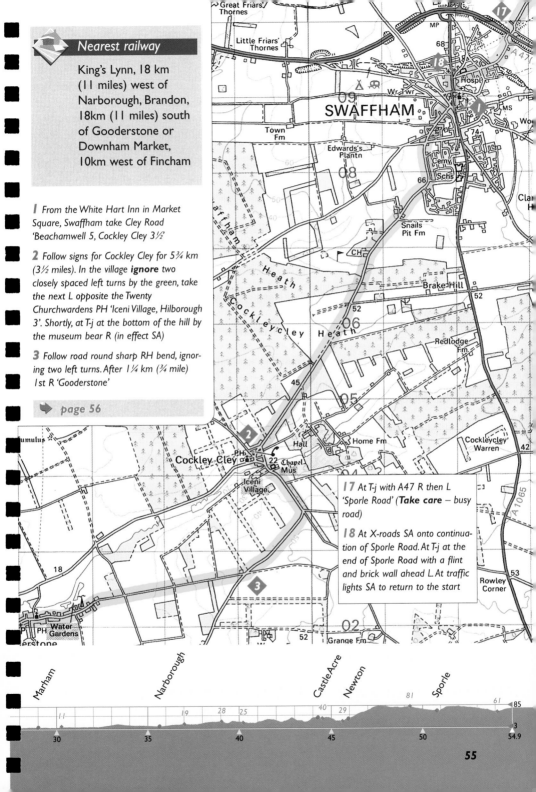

Nearest railway

King's Lynn, 18 km (11 miles) west of Narborough, Brandon, 18km (11 miles) south of Gooderstone or Downham Market, 10km west of Fincham

1 From the White Hart Inn in Market Square, Swaffham take Cley Road 'Beachamwell 5, Cockley Cley 3½'

2 Follow signs for Cockley Cley for 5¾ km (3½ miles). In the village **ignore** two closely spaced left turns by the green, take the next L opposite the Twenty Churchwardens PH 'Iceni Village, Hilborough 3'. Shortly, at T-j at the bottom of the hill by the museum bear R (in effect SA)

3 Follow road round sharp RH bend, ignoring two left turns. After 1¼ km (¾ mile) 1st R 'Gooderstone'

➡ page 56

17 At T-j with A47 R then L 'Sporle Road' (**Take care** – busy road)

18 At X-roads SA onto continuation of Sporle Road. At T-j at the end of Sporle Road with a flint and brick wall ahead L. At traffic lights SA to return to the start

55

4 Through Gooderstone. At X-roads L 'Oxborough'

5 Easy to miss. 3¼ km (2 miles) after passing Oxborough Hall, on a sharp LH bend shortly after crossing bridge over stream turn R 'Eastmoor, Beachamwell' then after ¾ km (½ mile) 1st L 'Boughton'

6 At T-j at the end of Oxborough Road bear R onto Chapel Road 'Barton Bendish, Fincham'

7 Through Boughton. 1¼ km (¾ mile) after the village pond 1st L on Gibbet Lane 'Wereham, Fincham' then shortly 1st R on

Fincham Road 'Fincham, Downham Market'

8 At X-roads with the A1122 in Fincham SA onto Marham Road 'Shouldam 2, Marham 2¾'

9 Views! At T-j at the bottom of the hill R 'Marham'

10 The next 9¾ km (6 miles) will have more traffic. Through Marham. After 4 km (2½ miles) at T-j L 'Narborough'

Places of interest

Swaffham 1
The town sign features local benefactor John Chapman, a 15th-century pedlar who found gold coins in his garden and gave money to the parish church. The Market Place is flanked by graceful 18th-century buildings, the Victorian Corn Exchange and old workshops

Cockley Cley 2
Reconstructed encampment of the Iceni tribe at the time of Queen Boudicca, with watch-towers, drawbridge, chariot house and snake pit, on the site of the original. The village contains the remains of a Saxon church

Oxburgh Hall 4-5
A red-brick, moated manor house, built in 1482 by the Bedingfield family, who still live there. There are tapestry panels embroidered by Mary, Queen of Scots, formal French gardens and views from the tower

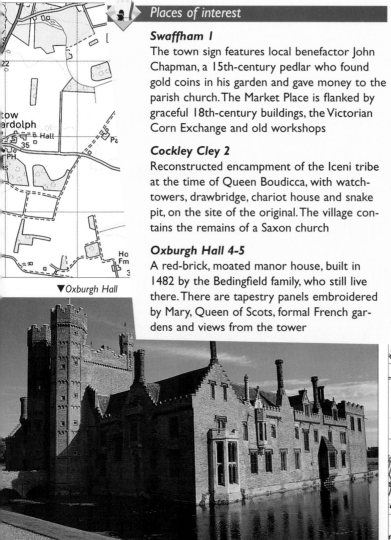

▼Oxburgh Hall

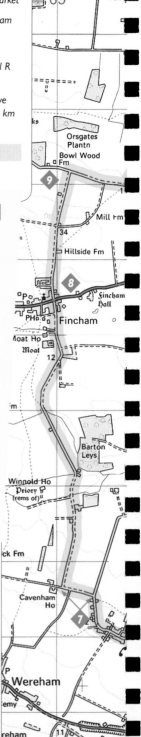

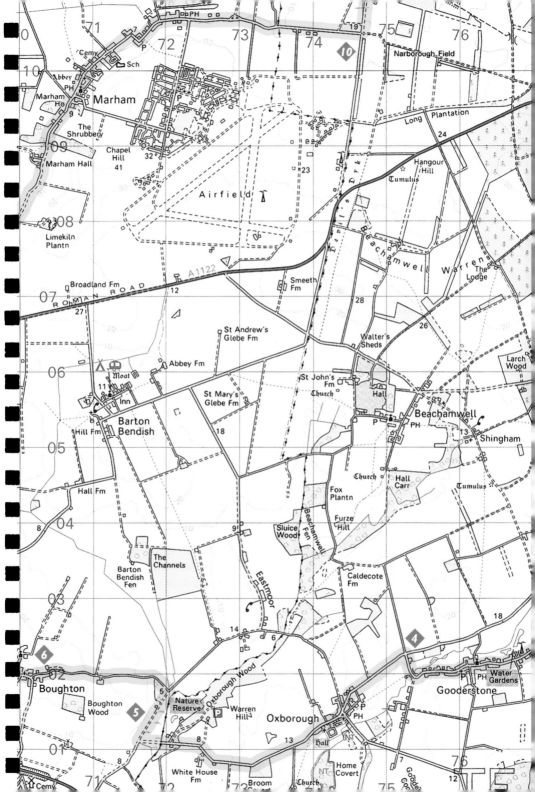

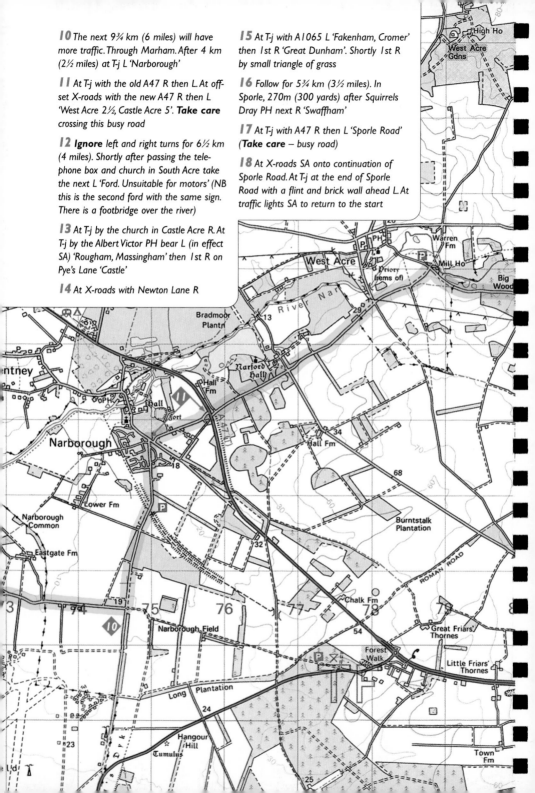

10 The next 9¾ km (6 miles) will have more traffic. Through Marham. After 4 km (2½ miles) at T-j L 'Narborough'

11 At T-j with the old A47 R then L. At off-set X-roads with the new A47 R then L 'West Acre 2½, Castle Acre 5'. **Take care** crossing this busy road

12 **Ignore** left and right turns for 6½ km (4 miles). Shortly after passing the telephone box and church in South Acre take the next L 'Ford. Unsuitable for motors' (NB this is the second ford with the same sign. There is a footbridge over the river)

13 At T-j by the church in Castle Acre R. At T-j by the Albert Victor PH bear L (in effect SA) 'Rougham, Massingham' then 1st R on Pye's Lane 'Castle'

14 At X-roads with Newton Lane R

15 At T-j with A1065 L 'Fakenham, Cromer' then 1st R 'Great Dunham'. Shortly 1st R by small triangle of grass

16 Follow for 5¾ km (3½ miles). In Sporle, 270m (300 yards) after Squirrels Dray PH next R 'Swaffham'

17 At T-j with A47 R then L 'Sporle Road' (**Take care** – busy road)

18 At X-roads SA onto continuation of Sporle Road. At T-j at the end of Sporle Road with a flint and brick wall ahead L. At traffic lights SA to return to the start

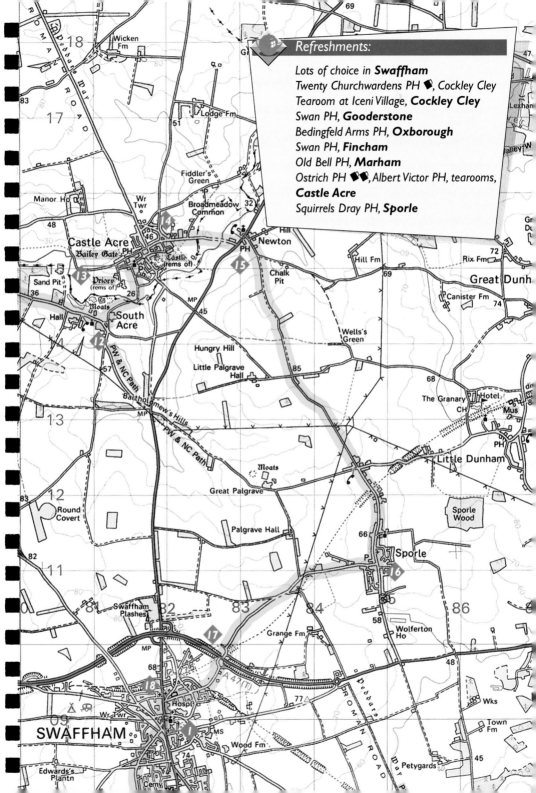

Refreshments:

Lots of choice in **Swaffham**
Twenty Churchwardens PH, Cockley Cley
Tearoom at Iceni Village, **Cockley Cley**
Swan PH, **Gooderstone**
Bedingfeld Arms PH, **Oxborough**
Swan PH, **Fincham**
Old Bell PH, **Marham**
Ostrich PH, Albert Victor PH, tearooms,
Castle Acre
Squirrels Dray PH, **Sporle**

North from East Dereham to Colkirk and the Wensum Valley

8

Start

The main square in East Dereham

P Follow signs

Distance and grade

50 km (31 miles)

Easy

Terrain

Gently undulating arable land, valley of the River Wensum. Lowest point – 16 m (53 feet) at crossing of River Wensum (17). Highest point – 80 m (265 feet) south of Whissonsett (6-7)

*T*he River Wensum rises to the south of Fakenham, the River Yare south of East Dereham; both rivers run eastwards, meeting just beyond Norwich, by which time they form the tidal River Yare. The Rivers Bure and the Waveney, the other two major rivers of east Norfolk, join the Yare to the east of Reedham and everything pours into the sea at Great Yarmouth. This ride runs north and west from East Dereham to the source of the River Wensum, near Whissonsett, passing the sand pits and lakes with their Canada geese near Longham.

You rarely get views in Norfolk, but from Dandy Farm, to the south of Whissonsett, there is a definite tree-fringed horizon if you look across the valley of the River Wensum. Soon after the ornate statues of the lodge house of Sennowe Hall, the best views of the river are to be had from the bridge over the old dismantled railway. North Elmham was the seat of the Bishop of 'North Folk' from AD 600 until it moved to Norwich, and the ruins of the Saxon cathedral and manor house can be seen just off the road. You cross the River Wensum twice; between the two crossings keep an eye out for the ruins of Bylaugh Hall up on the hill to your left (between 15 and 16). The ride turns south and west to return to East Dereham – the last two miles are the busiest of the ride.

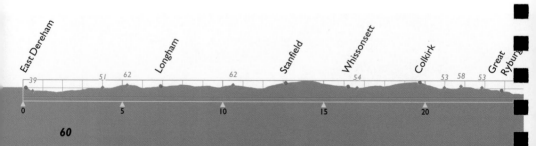

Wymondham, 18 km
(11 miles) southeast of
East Dereham

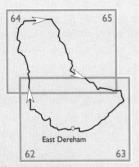

East Dereham

Places of interest

East Dereham 1
Site of the 7th-century nunnery founded by
St Withburga, now occupied by St
Nicholas' Church which is part Norman
with a 16th-century bell tower. The melan-
cholic poet William Cowper was buried
here in 1800. Bishop Bonner's Cottages,
with distinctive fruit-and-flower plasterwork, house an archaeological museum

Norfolk Rural Life Museum 2 miles north
of (3)
The complex, set in an 18th-century red-
brick workhouse, tells the story of village
life in past times with reconstructed workshops. Craftsmen's Row includes a smithy,
bakery and a village store

North Elmham 12
Seat of the Bishop of 'North Folk' from AD
600 until it moved to Norwich. The ruins
of the 11th-century Saxon cathedral and
1386 manor house blend in the moated
enclosure

Refreshments:

George PH ●, lots of choice
in **East Dereham**
White Horse PH, **Longham**
Swan Inn, **Whissonsett**
Crown Inn ●●, **Colkirk**
Boar Inn ●, **Great Ryburgh**
Kings Head PH ●, **North Elmham**
Darbys PH ●●, **Swanton Morley**
(1½ km (1 mile) south of 14)
Mermaid Inn, **Elsing**

▲ Bishop Bonner's Cottages, East Dereham

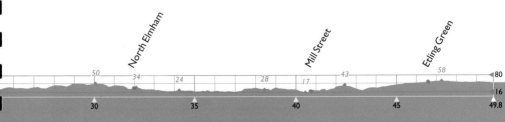

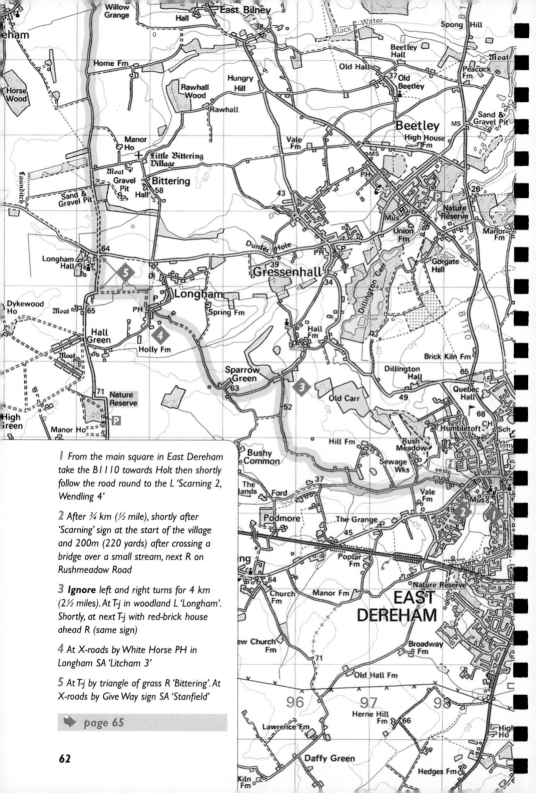

1 *From the main square in East Dereham take the B1110 towards Holt then shortly follow the road round to the L 'Scarning 2, Wendling 4'*

2 *After ¾ km (½ mile), shortly after 'Scarning' sign at the start of the village and 200m (220 yards) after crossing a bridge over a small stream, next R on Rushmeadow Road*

3 *Ignore left and right turns for 4 km (2½ miles). At T-j in woodland L 'Longham'. Shortly, at next T-j with red-brick house ahead R (same sign)*

4 *At X-roads by White Horse PH in Longham SA 'Litcham 3'*

5 *At T-j by triangle of grass R 'Bittering'. At X-roads by Give Way sign SA 'Stanfield'*

➡ *page 65*

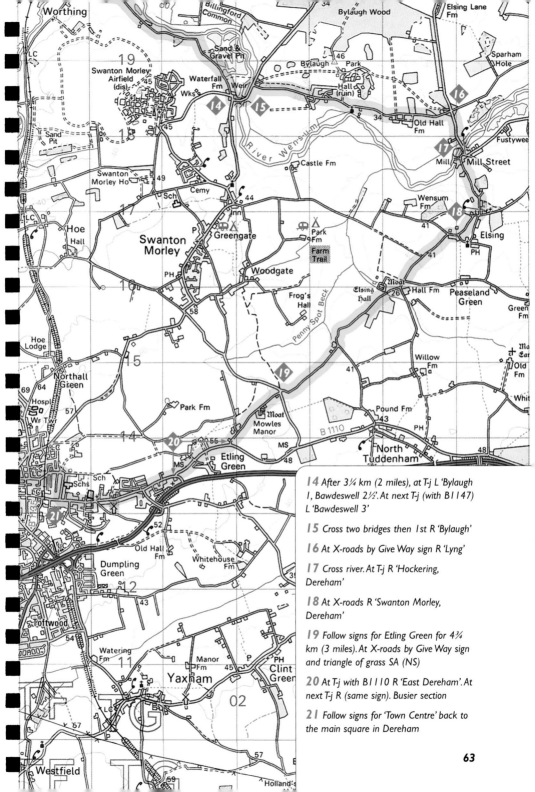

14 After 3¼ km (2 miles), at T-j L 'Bylaugh 1, Bawdeswell 2½'. At next T-j (with B1147) L 'Bawdeswell 3'

15 Cross two bridges then 1st R 'Bylaugh'

16 At X-roads by Give Way sign R 'Lyng'

17 Cross river. At T-j R 'Hockering, Dereham'

18 At X-roads R 'Swanton Morley, Dereham'

19 Follow signs for Etling Green for 4¾ km (3 miles). At X-roads by Give Way sign and triangle of grass SA (NS)

20 At T-j with B1110 R 'East Dereham'. At next T-j R (same sign). Busier section

21 Follow signs for 'Town Centre' back to the main square in Dereham

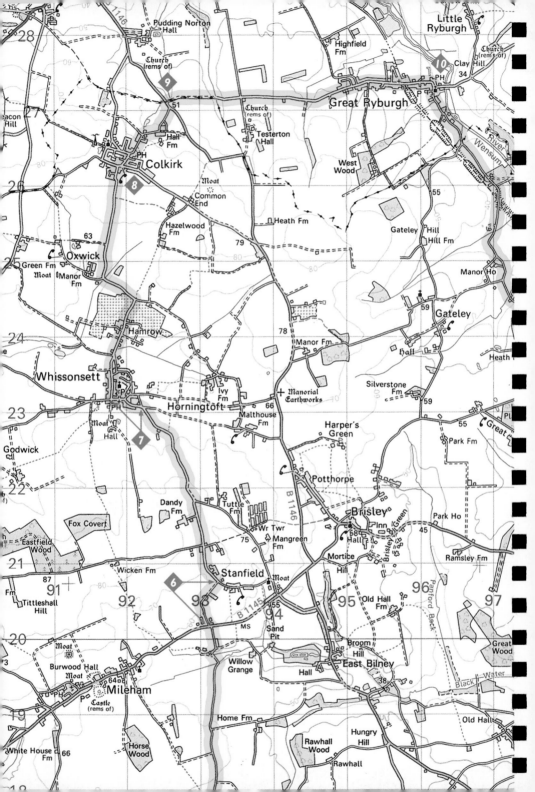

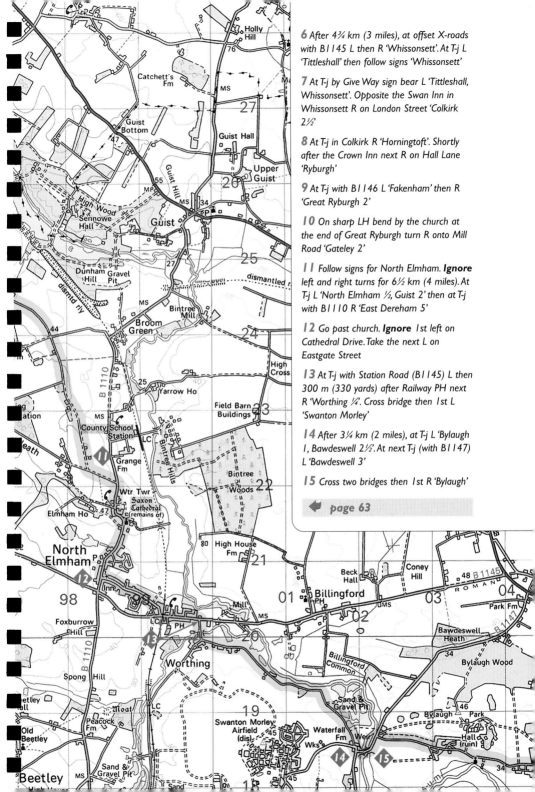

6 After 4¾ km (3 miles), at offset X-roads with B1145 L then R 'Whissonsett'. At T-j L 'Tittleshall' then follow signs 'Whissonsett'

7 At T-j by Give Way sign bear L 'Tittleshall, Whissonsett'. Opposite the Swan Inn in Whissonsett R on London Street 'Colkirk 2½'

8 At T-j in Colkirk R 'Horningtoft'. Shortly after the Crown Inn next R on Hall Lane 'Ryburgh'

9 At T-j with B1146 L 'Fakenham' then R 'Great Ryburgh 2'

10 On sharp LH bend by the church at the end of Great Ryburgh turn R onto Mill Road 'Gateley 2'

11 Follow signs for North Elmham. **Ignore** left and right turns for 6½ km (4 miles). At T-j L 'North Elmham ½, Guist 2' then at T-j with B1110 R 'East Dereham 5'

12 Go past church. **Ignore** 1st left on Cathedral Drive. Take the next L on Eastgate Street

13 At T-j with Station Road (B1145) L then 300 m (330 yards) after Railway PH next R 'Worthing ¼'. Cross bridge then 1st L 'Swanton Morley'

14 After 3¼ km (2 miles), at T-j L 'Bylaugh 1, Bawdeswell 2½'. At next T-j (with B1147) L 'Bawdeswell 3'

15 Cross two bridges then 1st R 'Bylaugh'

⬅ page 63

Southeast from Wroxham to the River Yare at Reedham

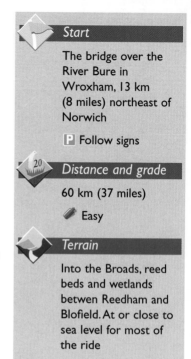

Start

The bridge over the River Bure in Wroxham, 13 km (8 miles) northeast of Norwich

P Follow signs

Distance and grade

60 km (37 miles)

Easy

Terrain

Into the Broads, reed beds and wetlands betwen Reedham and Blofield. At or close to sea level for most of the ride

The Norfolk Broads, a collection of reed-fringed lakes linked by the rivers Ant, Bure and Thurne, are without doubt best appreciated from a boat. Nevertheless, there are times when the network of lanes comes close to the water's edge, particularly at the Visitor Centre and Nature Trail at Ranworth Broad. Starting from Wroxham, the centre of boating activity in the Broads, the ride is unavoidably on busy roads for the first and last stretches. However, the outlook improves as the route swings east through the pretty, thatched village of Woodbastwick and the watery delights of Ranworth. Acle has little to detain you but Reedham is quite the opposite – it really feels as though it is a last outpost, with marshes and rivers acting as natural barriers on three sides and only a ferry carrying vehicles across the River Yare. There is the famous swing bridge for the railway, which opens to allow the passage of yachts and craft up the River Yare. West from here, careful attention should be paid to the instructions as there are several junctions to be navigated in order to stay as close as possible to the reed beds and the nature reserves near to the River Yare. Large conurbations, such as Norwich, have a habit of generating lots of traffic on all the roads within a few miles radius of the centre, even on minor roads, hence the meandering course through Panxworth to rejoin the outward route at Woodbastwick.

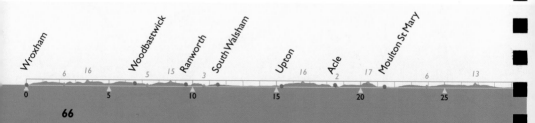

Nearest railway

Hoveton (Wroxham),
Acle or Reedham

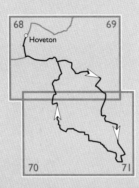

Refreshments:

Lots of choice in **Wroxham**
Fur & Feather PH 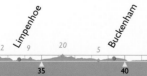, **Woodbastwick**
Maltsters PH, Granary Restaurant,
Ranworth
The Ship PH ❧, **South Walsham**
Kings Head PH, **Acle**
Ship PH, Lord Nelson PH, Railway Tavern
PH ❧, *tearooms,* **Reedham**
Kings Head PH, **Blofield**

Places of interest

Ranworth 5
A steep climb to the top of St Helen's
Church tower is rewarded with by vast
Broadland views. The glorious 15th-
century rood screen is painted with
saints, apostles and martyrs

Ranworth Broad 5
There is a boardwalk nature trail through
woodland and marshland to the floating
Broadland Conservation Centre, which
has displays explaining the history and
wildlife of Norfolk Broads, with a bird-
watching gallery upstairs

Reedham 15
A nautical village! The chain
ferry over the River Yare is the
only crossing for 42 km
(26 miles) between Norwich and
Great Yarmouth. The flint-walled
church stands aloof on a ridge
behind the village. There are exotic
birds at the nearby Animal Park

Strumpshaw Fen 22
Typical fenland country beside the
River Yare, with reed and sedge beds,
woodland, marshes and meadows rich
in birdlife which can be seen from a
network of foopaths and hides. The
Steam Museum has engines and a small
railway

▼ Ranworth Broad

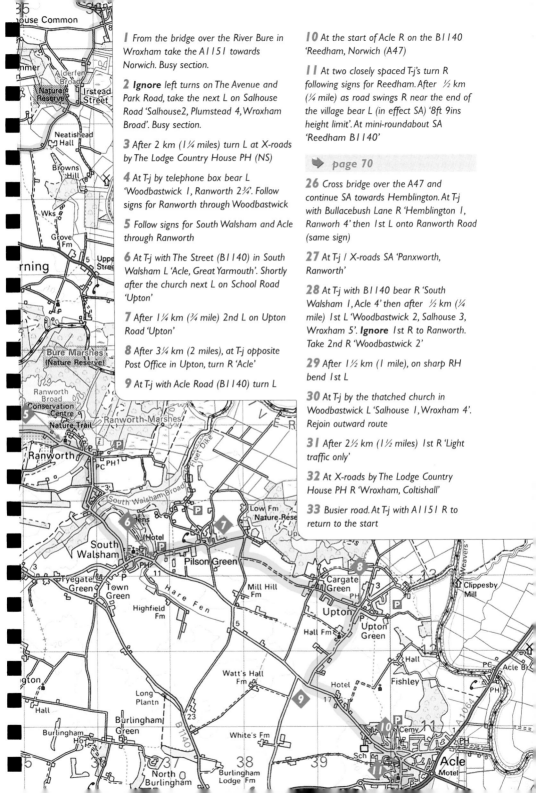

1 From the bridge over the River Bure in Wroxham take the A1151 towards Norwich. Busy section.

2 Ignore left turns on The Avenue and Park Road, take the next L on Salhouse Road 'Salhouse 2, Plumstead 4, Wroxham Broad'. Busy section.

3 After 2 km (1¼ miles) turn L at X-roads by The Lodge Country House PH (NS)

4 At T-j by telephone box bear L 'Woodbastwick 1, Ranworth 2¾. Follow signs for Ranworth through Woodbastwick

5 Follow signs for South Walsham and Acle through Ranworth

6 At T-j with The Street (B1140) in South Walsham L 'Acle, Great Yarmouth'. Shortly after the church next L on School Road 'Upton'

7 After 1¼ km (¾ mile) 2nd L on Upton Road 'Upton'

8 After 3¼ km (2 miles), at T-j opposite Post Office in Upton, turn R 'Acle'

9 At T-j with Acle Road (B1140) turn L

10 At the start of Acle R on the B1140 'Reedham, Norwich (A47)'

11 At two closely spaced T-j's turn R following signs for Reedham. After ½ km (¼ mile) as road swings R near the end of the village bear L (in effect SA) '8ft 9ins height limit'. At mini-roundabout SA 'Reedham B1140'

➡️ **page 70**

26 Cross bridge over the A47 and continue SA towards Hemblington. At T-j with Bullacebush Lane R 'Hemblington 1, Ranworh 4' then 1st L onto Ranworth Road (same sign)

27 At T-j / X-roads SA 'Panxworth, Ranworth'

28 At T-j with B1140 bear R 'South Walsham 1, Acle 4' then after ½ km (¼ mile) 1st L 'Woodbastwick 2, Salhouse 3, Wroxham 5'. **Ignore** 1st R to Ranworth. Take 2nd R 'Woodbastwick 2'

29 After 1½ km (1 mile), on sharp RH bend 1st L

30 At T-j by the thatched church in Woodbastwick L 'Salhouse 1, Wroxham 4'. Rejoin outward route

31 After 2½ km (1½ miles) 1st R 'Light traffic only'

32 At X-roads by The Lodge Country House PH R 'Wroxham, Coltishall'

33 Busier road. At T-j with A1151 R to return to the start

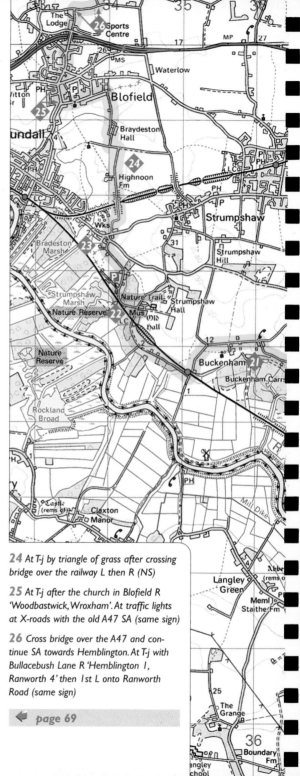

11 At two closely spaced T-j's turn R following signs for Reedham. After ½ km (¼ mile) as road swings R near the end of the village bear L (in effect SA) '8ft 9ins height limit'. At mini-roundabout SA 'Reedham B1140'

12 Easy to miss. After 4¾ km (3 miles) 1st proper L onto Halvergate Road 'Halvergate 1¼, Great Yarmouth'

13 At T-j at the end of Moulton Road R 'Freethorpe' then shortly, on sharp RH bend, bear L

14 After 5¾ km (3½ miles), by the car park for Animal Adventure Park, turn R on Church Road 'Reedham Village Centre' then after ¾ km (½ mile) 1st L (same sign)

15 Follow the road through Reedham. At T-j with Station Road by the memorial stone L. At T-j by the railway station R 'Freethorpe'

16 Ignore 1st left on Station Drive. After ¾ km (½ mile) next L 'Limpenhoe 1'

17 At junction by farm R then L onto Reedham Road 'Limpenhoe'

18 At T-j by triangle of grass with a five-windowed house ahead turn R then shortly at next T-j at the end of Reedham Road L towards the church

19 After the church, follow the road around to the R then 1st L onto Cantley Road 'Cantley'

20 At X-roads SA 'Lingwood'. **Easy to miss.** Follow the road round to the R then after ¾ km (½ mile), immediately after a large thatched, red-brick barn on the left take the next L (NS)

21 At T-j by letter box L (NS). After ¾ km (½ mile) 1st L onto no through road 'Buckenham Railway Staion'. Cross railway line and turn R

22 Shortly after the next railway crossing 1st L (NS) opposite thatched red-brick barns

23 At T-j at the end of Low Road L. Shortly, at next T-j R then L (NS)

24 At T-j by triangle of grass after crossing bridge over the railway L then R (NS)

25 At T-j after the church in Blofield R 'Woodbastwick, Wroxham'. At traffic lights at X-roads with the old A47 SA (same sign)

26 Cross bridge over the A47 and continue SA towards Hemblington. At T-j with Bullacebush Lane R 'Hemblington 1, Ranworth 4' then 1st L onto Ranworth Road (same sign)

← page 69

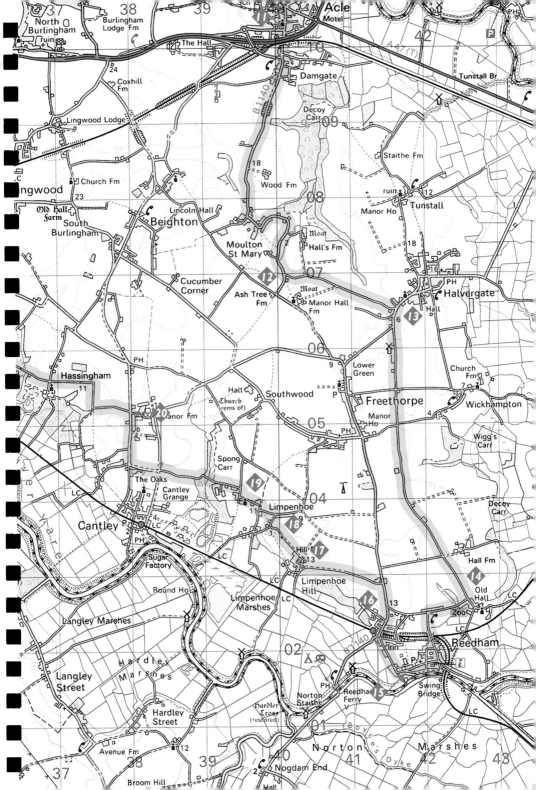

10 Along the Yare valley from Norwich to Loddon

Start

Bonds Shopping Centre in Norwich

P If arriving by car, it is better to park at (3) at the bottom of Long John Hill, starting and finishing the ride here

Distance and grade

51 km (32 miles)

Easy

Terrain

River valley, reed beds, gently undulating arable land. Lowest point – sea level at several points along the Waveney valley. Highest point – 65m (213 feet) at Upper Stoke (22)

Norwich has a fairly enlightened attitude towards cycling, and to the northwest of the city there is an excellent track known as the Marriotts Way which has been created from a dismantled railway starting near the city centre and running for several miles to Reepham. This is described fully in off-road route 4. To the southeast of Norwich there are two much shorter sections of dedicated cyclepath which help you out of the city and over the A47, avoiding main roads. There are lovely views of the River Yare near to Kirby Bedon complete with pleasure boats and anglers. This is followed by what must be one of the steepest hills in Norfolk! There are many attractive old red-brick barns and buildings, some with thatched roofs. Try not to miss the ruins of the castle and the manor house at Claxton. Down on the marshes, cattle graze during the summer months. The tidal creek at Hardley Flood on the River Chet just beyond Langley Street reminds you how far inland the sea affects the water levels. There is an unusual thatched tower on the church in Chedgrave and many fine old buildings of brick and flint around the handsome square in Loddon. On the return route to Norwich, every attempt is made to avoid the busier lanes and roads that draw traffic into the region's capital.

Norwich — Trowse Newton — Bramerton — Surlingham — Rockland St Mary — Langley Green — Langley Street

10   33   3   15   6   10

0   5   10   15   20   25

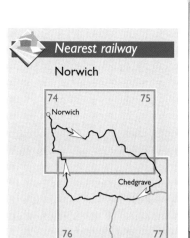

74	75
Norwich	
	Chedgrave
76	77

▶ *Norwich Cathedral*

Lots of choice in **Norwich**
Woods End Tavern, **Woods End**
New Inn, **Rockland**
Beauchamp Arms PH, near **Claxton**
The Wherry PH, **Langley Green**
White Horse PH, **Chedgrave**
Swan PH , Angel PH, Fox & Hounds
PH, **Loddon**
The Globe PH, **Shotesham**

Places of interest

Norwich 1

East Anglia's flourishing capital has one of the country's most beautiful cathedrals, started in 1094. The nave roof and cloisters have bosses painted with Biblical scenes and grotesque creatures. The city centre has some 30 medieval churches and is dominated by Norwich Castle which houses a military museum. There are death masks of executed prisoners in the dungeons. Museums abound: there are archaeology and art galleries in the castle; the medieval Stranger's Hall has period rooms depicting domestic life from Tudor to Victorian times

Chedgrave
Loddon   Mundham   Seething   Kirstead Hall   Shotesham   Upper Stroke

15   20   33   42   39   43   25   10   65
       30   35   40   45   50   51.0   0

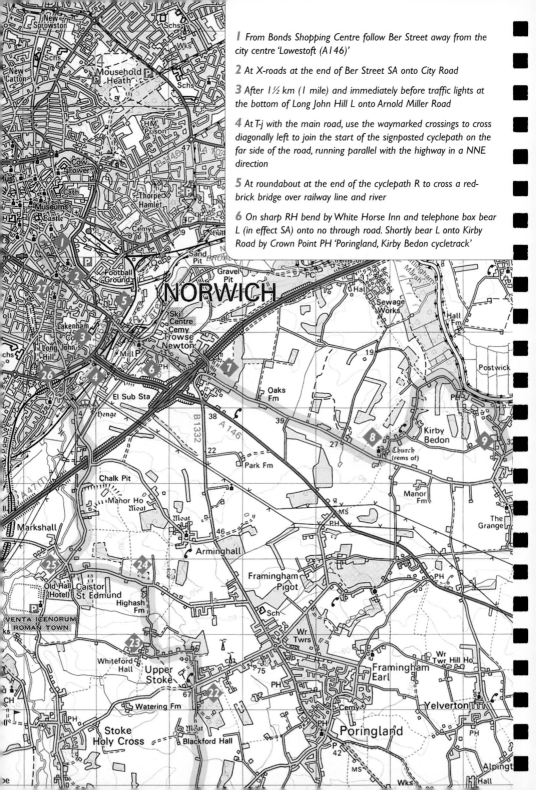

1 *From Bonds Shopping Centre follow Ber Street away from the city centre 'Lowestoft (A146)'*

2 *At X-roads at the end of Ber Street SA onto City Road*

3 *After 1½ km (1 mile) and immediately before traffic lights at the bottom of Long John Hill L onto Arnold Miller Road*

4 *At T-j with the main road, use the waymarked crossings to cross diagonally left to join the start of the signposted cyclepath on the far side of the road, running parallel with the highway in a NNE direction*

5 *At roundabout at the end of the cyclepath R to cross a red-brick bridge over railway line and river*

6 *On sharp RH bend by White Horse Inn and telephone box bear L (in effect SA) onto no through road. Shortly bear L onto Kirby Road by Crown Point PH 'Poringland, Kirby Bedon cycletrack'*

7 Follow signs for Kirby Bedon. Cross bridge over A47. At T-j L 'Kirby Bedon'

8 After 4 km (2½ miles), having ignored left turn to water treatment works, 1st proper L onto The Street 'Wood End 1'

9 Follow the lane alongside river, climb steeply, at T-j by triangle of grass L 'Surlingham 1½'

10 Into Surlingham. Towards the end of the village turn R by triangle of grass onto Mill Road 'Rockland 1½, Claxton 3'

11 At T-j at the end of Surlingham Lane L 'Claxton 1½, Langley 3¾'

12 After 6½ km (4 miles), on sharp RH bend by memorial cross and The Wherry PH, bear L (in effect SA) onto Langley Street 'Langley Street ½, Hardley 2'

➡ **page 76**

22 After 4 km (2½ miles), at X-roads by Give Way sign and telephone box in Upper Stoke SA 'Caistor St Edmund, Trowse'

23 Go round sharp LH bend then after ¾ km (½ mile) 1st R 'Valley Farm Lane. 7.5 ton weight limit'

24 At T-j at the end of High Ash Lane L (NS)

25 At X-roads by Give Way sign R 'Arninghall'

26 Busier section. Cross the A47. At traffic lights SA onto Long John Hill to rejoin outward route

27 At X-roads with Bracondale at the end of City Road SA onto Ber Street to return to the start

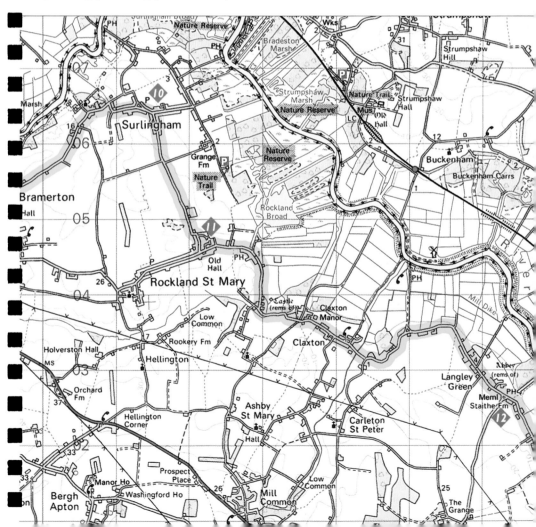

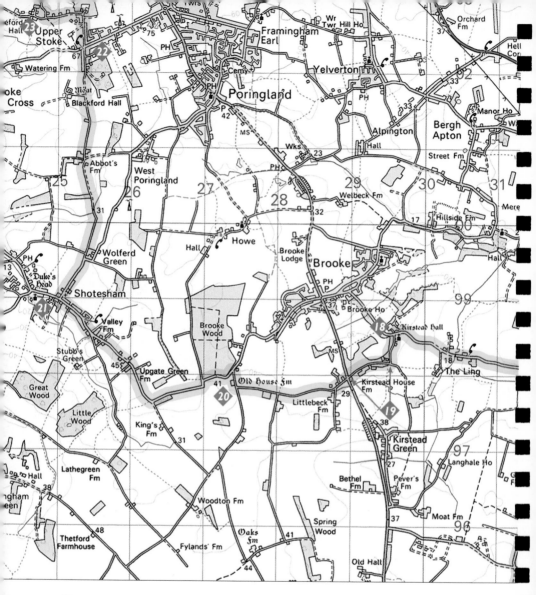

12 After 6½ km (4 miles), on sharp RH bend by memorial cross and The Wherry PH, bear L (in effect SA) onto Langley Street 'Langley Street ½, Hardley 2'

13 At T-j with Cross Stone Road by small red-brick bus shelter turn R 'Carleton St Peter 2½, Loddon 1¾'

14 After ¾ km (½ mile) at the next T-j R 'Loddon 1¼, Chedgrave 1'

15 At X-roads at the end of Hardley Road L 'Loddon

¼'. At T-j by White Horse PH in Chedgrave turn L

16 Cross bridge then 1st R just past Kings Head PH in Loddon 'Seething 3½, Brooke 5½'

17 At offset X-roads with A146 R then L 'Mundham 2¼, Sisland ½'

18 Through Mundham and Seething. **Easy to miss.** 3¼ km (2 miles) after Seething Church L onto Church Road by the square-towered flint church at Kirstead

19 *After ½ km (¼ mile), on sharp LH bend (Zig Zag Lane) turn R 'Brooke 1¼'. At X-roads (with B1332) by Give Way sign SA onto Littlebeck Lane*

20 *At T-j at the end of Mill Lane R 'Brooke 1½, Shotesham 1½' then shortly, at T-j with High Green L 'Shotesham 1½'*

21 *Easy to miss. ¾ km (½ mile) after the 'Shotesham' sign at the start of the village, next R onto Chapel Lane 'Poringland 2½'. After ¾ km*

(½ mile), on sharp RH bend bear L (in effect SA) 'Stoke Holy Cross 2'

22 *After 4 km (2½ miles), at X-roads by Give Way sign and telephone box in Upper Stoke SA 'Caistor St Edmund, Trowse'*

23 *Go round sharp LH bend then after ¾ km .½ mile) 1st R 'Valley Farm Lane. 7.5 ton weight limit'*

◀ page 75

The marshlands of the River Waveney northeast of Bungay

This ride, together with the one starting from Norwich, explores the triangle of land lying between the Rivers Yare and Waveney. The rides meet at the village of Loddon and it is possible to make a 113-km (70-mile) loop by linking the two together. The ride starts by heading southwest from the attractive town of Bungay, and you may wish to visit the Otter Trust, which lies less than a mile off the route beyond Earsham, at the start of the ride. The imposing façade of Earsham Hall is the first of several fine houses passed along the course of the route; the next is at the crossroads with the B1332 near the Mermaid PH south of Hedenham. Flint churches punctuate a gently undulating countryside dedicated to arable farming and occasional broadleaf woodland. Loddon has a fine square at its heart, with an ornate flint library standing on one side and further handsome red-brick buildings clustered close to the centre of the village. The flint church at Heckingham has a hexagonal tower with thatch. Beyond here the ride passes east into the marshland that lies to the north and south of the River Waveney. The ride then heads back west towards Bungay along lanes just to the north of the River Waveney which, for much of its length, forms the boundary between Norfolk and Suffolk.

▶ *Spink's Hill church, north of Ditchingham*

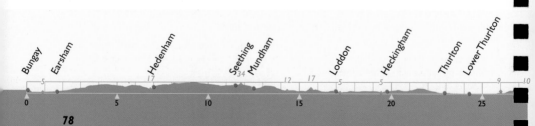

Nearest railway

Beccles, 3 km (2 miles) south of the route at 16 / 17 or Haddiscoe Station, 3 km (2 miles) north of the route at 11

Refreshments:

Green Dragon PH 🍺, lots of choice in **Bungay**
Mermaid PH, **Hedenham**
Swan PH 🍺, Angel PH, Fox & Hounds PH, **Loddon**
Queens Head PH, **Thurlton**
Crown Inn 🍺, **Haddiscoe**
Waveney Inn, **Staithe**

Places of interest

Bungay 1
The village is dominated by the stone towers of the 12th-century castle gatehouse and the pinnacle of the 12th-century church of St Mary, part of a Benedictine nunnery whose ruined walls are visible in the churchyard. The elegant 18th-century houses were built after a fire in 1688

Bungay Otter Trust (near 1)
The otters are in near-natural surroundings beside the River Waveney at Earsham and have been bred to protect the species from extinction. There are woods, lakes with abundant waterfowl, a night heronry and a nature trail

Raveningham Gardens 3km (2 miles) south of the route at 7-8
There are rare plants, shrubs and trees in the gardens surrounding the elegant Georgian house

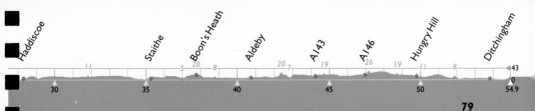

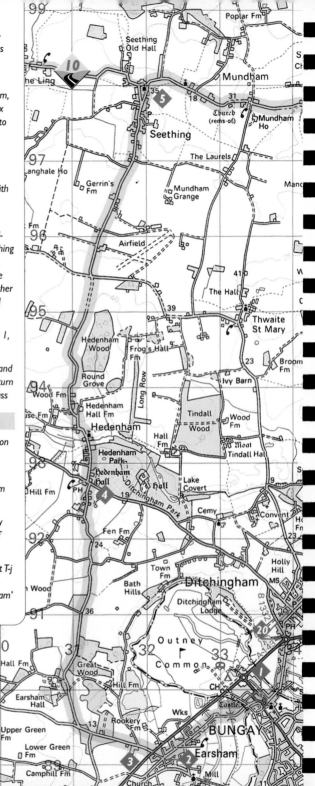

1 *From the Kings Hotel near the round-about in the heart of Bungay follow signs for Earsham along the Earsham Road*

2 Easy to miss. *After 1½ km (1 mile), towards the end of the village of Earsham, 180m (200 yards) after a telephone box on the left, turn R by memorial cross onto no through road by Queens Head PH*

3 *At X-roads with A143 SA 'Hedenham 3¼, Bedingham, Topcroft'*

4 *After 4¾ km (3 miles), at X-roads (with B1332) at the end of Earsham Road L then R onto Church Road*

5 *After 6½ km (4 miles), at T-j by round-towered, flint and thatch church in Seething turn R onto Loddon Road 'Mundham ¾, Loddon 2¾' [***Or** for link to Norwich ride turn L 'Kirstead 1½, Brooke 2', do the other ride and rejoin this ride at instruction 7]*

6 *After 4 km (2½ miles), at offset X-roads with A146 R then L 'Chedgrave 1, Loddon ¼'*

7 *At T-j in Loddon R. Go past Angel PH and Fox & Hounds PH. On sharp RH bend turn L onto Norton Road by a triangle of grass*

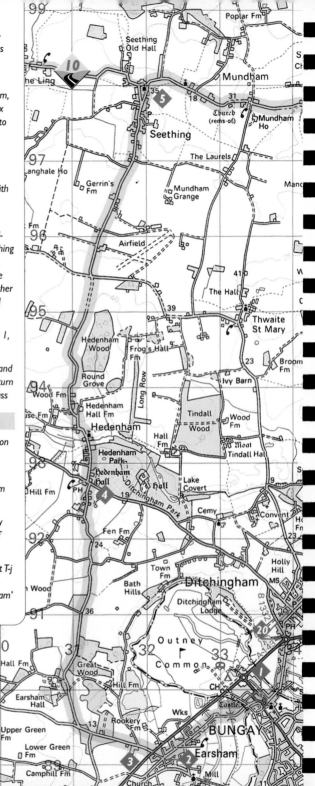

17 *At X-roads (with B1140) SA 'Stockton ½, Kirby Cane 2¾'*

18 *At X-roads (with A146) SA onto Bungay Road 'Ditchingham 3, Hedenham 4'*

19 *Follow signs for Broome and Bungay for 4¾ km (3 miles). At T-j at the end of Bungay Road bear L (in effect SA)*

20 *At X-roads SA onto Loddon Road. At T-j with B1332 L 'Bungay 1' then at round-about 2nd exit 'Wainford Mill, Mettingham' to return to the start*

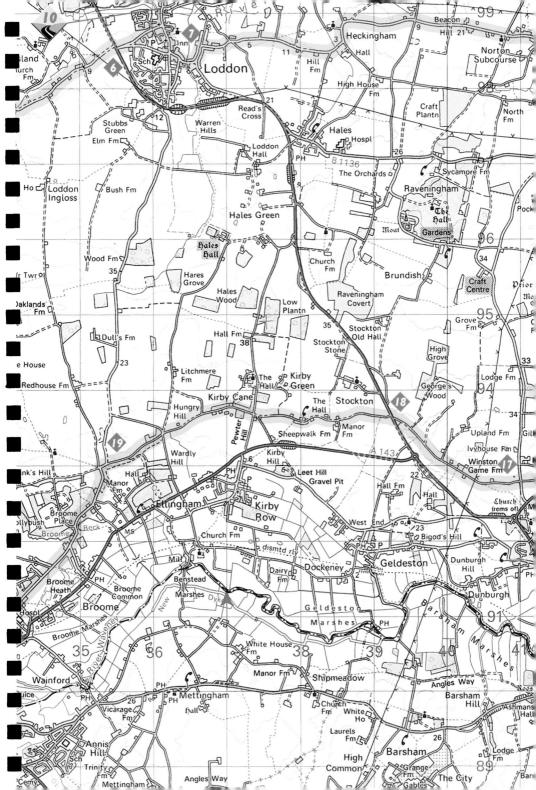

8 After 5¾ km (3½ miles) at T-j with B1140 in Thurlton bear R (in effect SA) 'Gillingham 4¾, Haddiscoe 2¼'

9 Shortly, cross bridge then on sharp RH bend by the Queens Head PH in Thurlton bear L (in effect SA) then 1st L 'Lower Thurlton 1, Marshes'

10 After 3¼ km (2 miles), at T-j by round-towered church L 'Haddiscoe'

11 At T-j (with A143) by the Crown Inn in Haddiscoe R then 1st L onto Wiggs Road 'Aldeby 2½, Burgh St Peter 3'

12 Easy to miss. After 3¼ km (2 miles), shortly after a sharp RH bend 1st L 'Waveney River Centre, Burgh St Peter 2, Staithe'

13 After 4 km (2½ miles), follow the road round to the R by the Waveney Inn. **Ignore** the 1st left on Dick's Mount. Take the next L on Grays Road 'Marshes'

14 At T-j by Give Way sign at the end of Grays Road L

15 After 3¼ km (2 miles), at T-j by thatched bus shelter L 'Beccles 4' then shortly at next T-j L (same sign)

16 At T-j with A143 L 'Diss, Beccles', then after 1¼ km (¾ mile) 1st R by triangle of grass (NS)

17 At X-roads (with B1140) SA 'Stockton ½, Kirby Cane 2¾'

18 At X-roads (with A146) SA onto Bungay Road 'Ditchingham 3, Hedenham 4'

◀ page 80

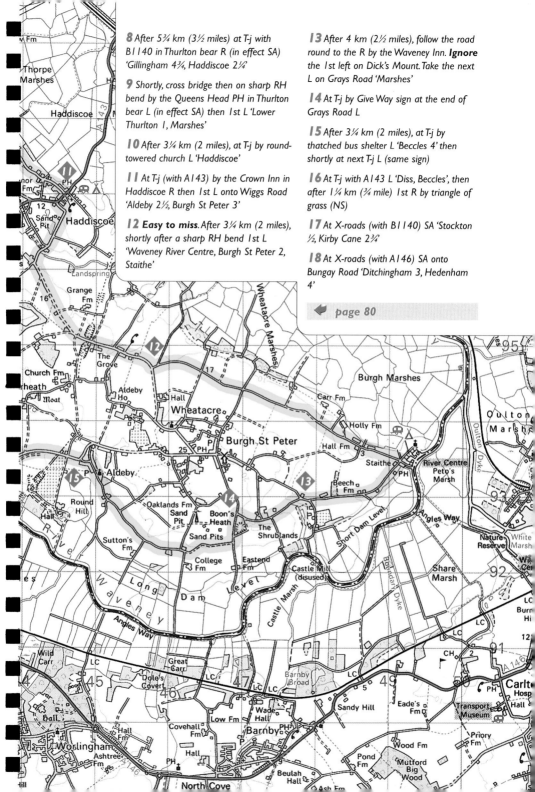

12 Southeast from Beccles to the coast at Southwold

This ride is one of three that explore Suffolk rather than Norfolk or Cambridgeshire. The attractive town of Beccles has one of the most confusing one-way systems in the region, hence the amount of instruction needed to guide you out of town to the start of the curiously named Cucumber Lane and into the heart of the Suffolk countryside. On its way southeast to the coast, the ride runs through gently undulating arable land. There are occasional pockets of permanent pasture and woodland, with trees particularly in evidence around the estate of Sotterley Hall. You will pass flint churches and red-brick houses and barns, normally with red tiles but occasionally thatched. Covehithe has two outstanding curiosities: a road which is gradually retreating before the onslaught of the sea, and a small thatched church built within the ruins of a much larger church. The last 2–3 miles of the ride into Southwold are busy and unavoidable. The charms of this seaside town and its many fine taverns should be recompense for the unwelcome volume of traffic – if you can, avoid fine weekends in the summer when the roads are likely to be at their busiest. On your return journey to Beccles, keep an eye out for the intricate stonework on the church at Stoven.

Start

St Michael's Church tower in the centre of Beccles, 17 miles southeast of Norwich

P Free parking near Tourist Information Centre, follow signs

Distance and grade

51 km (32 miles)

Easy

Terrain

Arable land with some broadleaf woodland between Beccles and the coast. Crumbling coastline at Covehithe. Lowest point – sea level at Southwold. Highest point – 36m (118 ft) between Brampton railway station and Beccles

Beccles Ellough 20 Wrentham Covehithe South Cove 12 13 Cove Bottom 11 10

0   5   10   15   20

86		87
Beccles○		
88	Southwold	89

▼ Southwold

Places of interest

Beccles 1
Mellow old town on the River Waveney with handsome red-brick Georgian houses. The best-preserved are in Ballygate and Northgate. Gardens run down to the waterside, which is fringed with boat-houses

Southwold 16
Once a Saxon fishing port and now a charming seaside town. Set around nine greens, there are period houses and Dutch-gabled cottages, many painted in pinks and pale blues. The white-washed 1890 lighthouse can be seen from all over town. A ship's figurehead stands outside Park Lane Cottage; there are more in the Sailors' Reading Room in East Street. The Perpendicular Church of St Edmund houses 'Southwold Jack', a 15th-century mechanical figure of an armoured foot soldier. When a cord is pulled, his battleaxe strikes a bell

Refreshments:

Lots of choice in **Beccles**
Crown PH 🍴🍴, lots of choice in
Southwold
Angel PH 🍴🍴, **Wangford**
Cherry Tree PH, **Stoven**
Dog Inn 🍴, **Brampton**

Southwold · Reydon · Wangford · Stoven · Brampton · Brampton Station · Ringsfield Corner

6   6   10   16   36

30   35   40   45   50 50.7

85

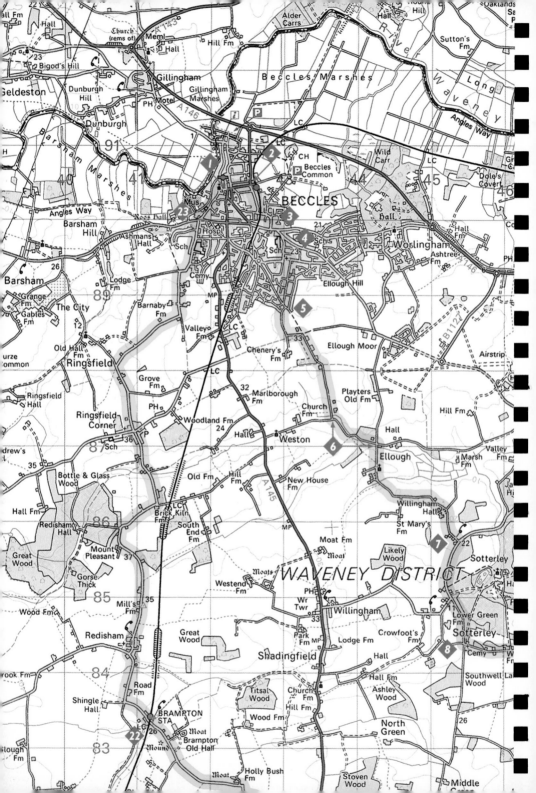

1 From the T-j near St Michael's church-tower in the centre of Beccles, follow signs for Ipswich and Lowestoft, bearing L along Market Street and SA at two sets of traffic lights

2 At mini-roundabout at the end of Station Road by railway station turn R onto Gosford Road

3 Cross railway line. At T-j at the end of Grove Road, L then 1st R onto B1127 (Ellough Road) 'Hulver' and immediately R again onto Castle Hill

4 Take the 3rd L onto Coney Hill then 1st R onto Banham Road

5 Once again, 3rd L onto Oak Lane then immediately R onto Cucumber Lane

6 At T-j at the end of Cucumber Lane L. After 1¼ km (¾ mile) 1st R at X-roads 'Sotterley 1¾, Southwold 9'

7 At T-j by triangle of grass with oak tree turn R 'Sotterley ¾, Wangford 4½'

8 After 1½ km (1 mile) L at X-roads by memorial cross 'Wrentham 3½, Henstead 2½'

9 At T-j with telephone box ahead R 'Wrentham 2½, Southwold 6¾'. After 1¼ km (¾ mile) follow road round sharp LH bend

10 At X-roads by church and large, attractive thatched house SA 'Wrentham B1127' then 1st L onto Priory Road

11 At X-roads (with A12) SA onto lane opposite. After ½ km (¼ mile) 1st R (NS) opposite thatched wooden barns to the left then at T-j L (NS)

➡ **page 88**

22 After 3¼ km (2 miles) cross the railway line. At T-j 1¼ km (¾ mile) after the railway crossing R 'Ringsfield 3, Beccles 4½'

23 **Ignore** left and right turnings for 6½ km (4 miles). At X-roads at the end of Ringsfield Road on the outskirts of Beccles SA onto Ballygate 'Town Centre' and follow back to the start

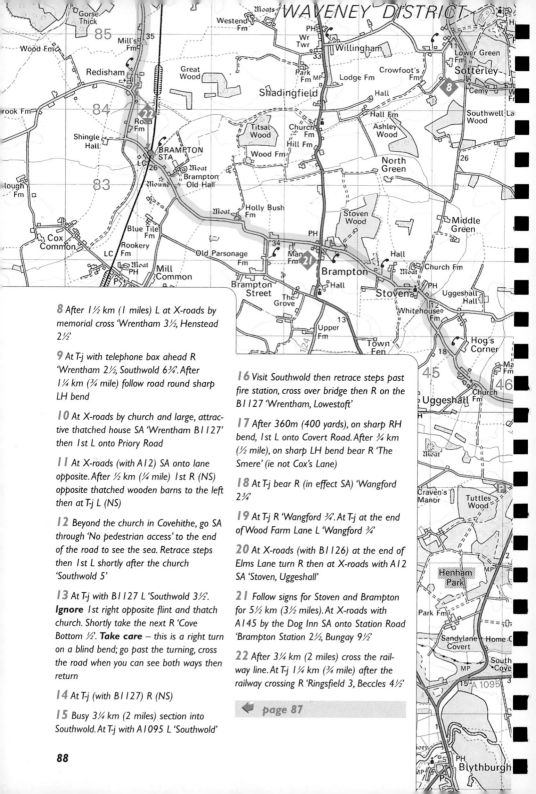

8 After 1½ km (1 miles) L at X-roads by memorial cross 'Wrentham 3½, Henstead 2½'

9 At T-j with telephone box ahead R 'Wrentham 2½, Southwold 6¾'. After 1¼ km (¾ mile) follow road round sharp LH bend

10 At X-roads by church and large, attractive thatched house SA 'Wrentham B1127' then 1st L onto Priory Road

11 At X-roads (with A12) SA onto lane opposite. After ½ km (¼ mile) 1st R (NS) opposite thatched wooden barns to the left then at T-j L (NS)

12 Beyond the church in Covehithe, go SA through 'No pedestrian access' to the end of the road to see the sea. Retrace steps then 1st L shortly after the church 'Southwold 5'

13 At T-j with B1127 L 'Southwold 3½'. **Ignore** 1st right opposite flint and thatch church. Shortly take the next R 'Cove Bottom ½'. **Take care** – this is a right turn on a blind bend; go past the turning, cross the road when you can see both ways then return

14 At T-j (with B1127) R (NS)

15 Busy 3¼ km (2 miles) section into Southwold. At T-j with A1095 L 'Southwold'

16 Visit Southwold then retrace steps past fire station, cross over bridge then R on the B1127 'Wrentham, Lowestoft'

17 After 360m (400 yards), on sharp RH bend, 1st L onto Covert Road. After ¾ km (½ mile), on sharp LH bend bear R 'The Smere' (ie not Cox's Lane)

18 At T-j bear R (in effect SA) 'Wangford 2¾'

19 At T-j R 'Wangford ¾'. At T-j at the end of Wood Farm Lane L 'Wangford ¾'

20 At X-roads (with B1126) at the end of Elms Lane turn R then at X-roads with A12 SA 'Stoven, Uggeshall'

21 Follow signs for Stoven and Brampton for 5½ km (3½ miles). At X-roads with A145 by the Dog Inn SA onto Station Road 'Brampton Station 2½, Bungay 9½'

22 After 3¼ km (2 miles) cross the railway line. At T-j 1¼ km (¾ mile) after the railway crossing R 'Ringsfield 3, Beccles 4½'

◀ page 87

▲ Crumbling coast-
line at Covehithe

13 From Harleston through the 'Saints' to Laxfield and Hoxne

Start

Magpie Hotel, near the clocktower in Harleston, on the A143 between Bury St Edmunds and Lowestoft

P Follow signs

Distance and grade

60 kms (37 miles)

Easy

The River Waveney marks the boundary between the counties of Norfolk and Suffolk for much of its length. Harleston lies just north of the river and is therefore in Norfolk; with the exception of a few minutes at the start and finish, the ride is south of the river and lies in Suffolk. The ride descends from the attractive market town of Harleston to cross the Waveney before passing through the area known as 'The Saints': there are no fewer than ten villages or hamlets with 'Saint' in their name. Beyond Rumburgh the land drains gently to the southeast into the River Blythe which reaches the sea near Southwold.

There is an unusual red-brick tower on the church at Ubbeston – almost all the churches in the area are made of flint. Just beyond here a beautiful panoply of trees arches over the narrow lane. The ride turns northeast along the valley of the Waveney (keep an eye out for Monk's Hall to the left, 2 miles after leaving Hoxne). The climb back up from the river to Harleston is the least welcome of the day, but at least you have been warned!

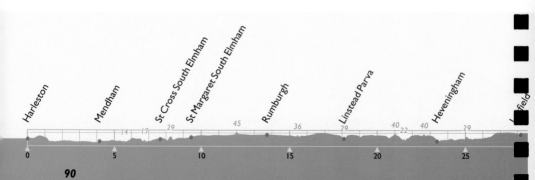

Terrain

Valley of the River
Waveney, undulating
arable famland with
broadleaf copses.
Attractive villages of
old red brick and flint.
Lowest point – 13m
(45 ft) in the Waveney
valley just north of
Mendham. Highest
point – 60m (197 ft)
just east of Wilby

Nearest railway

Halesworth, 5 km
(3 miles) southeast of
the route near
Rumburgh (8)

Places of interest

Heveningham Hall 1½ km (1 mile) east
of Huntingfield (9-10)
Georgian mansion built in 1780 as the
Vanneck family home. The exterior was
designed by Sir Robert Taylor. The inte-
rior, by James Wyatt, contains some of
his best surviving work. The grounds
were laid out by 'Capability' Brown

Eye 5 km (3 miles) west of the route at 18
Once an island town, it was granted a
charter by King John in 1205. The
Norman Castle was demolished in 1655
by Cromwell's army; the stones were
used to make a 19th-century folly. The
15th-century church has a fine rood
screen and a flint-and-stone tower. The
are fine 18th-century houses and a
16th-century Guildhall

Refreshments

Lots of choice in **Harleston**
Sir Alfred Munnings PH 🍷, **Mendham**
Rumburgh Buck PH 🍷, **Rumburgh**
Kings Head PH 🍷🍷, *Royal Oak PH,* **Laxfield**
Church Cottage Pottery Tea Shop, **Wilby**
Swan PH 🍷, **Hoxne**

Wilby · 58 · 43 · 55 · Horham · Denham · 41 · Hoxne · 40 · 20 · Shotford Heath · 37 · 60 · 13

30 · 35 · 40 · 45 · 50 · 55 · 57.1

1 With back to the Magpie Hotel in Harleston turn L 'All other routes'

2 Follow signs for Halesworth (B1116 and B1123). At the end of Harleston turn L onto Shotford Road 'Metfield 6, Fressingfield 6'

3 **Easy to miss.** Pass beneath A143. At the bottom of the hill, just before the bridge over the river turn L (NS)

4 After 3¼ km (2 miles) 1st R at X-roads (your priority) by triangle of grass 'Mendham ¼'

5 Cross bridge over river, go past Sir Alfred Munnings PH. At X-roads L 'Homersfield 3'

6 Cross bridge over small stream. Climb hill, **ignore** right turn to Middleton Hall. take the next R on a LH bend 'St Cross ¾'

7 At T-j by triangle of grass L 'Homersfield 1½, Harleston 4¾' then shortly at next T-j R 'Halesworth, St Margaret South Elmham'

8 Follow signs for Rumburgh and Halesworth for 8 km (5 miles), passing through St Margaret and Rumburgh. **Easy to miss.** 2½ km (1½ miles) after the Rumburgh Buck PH turn R 'Chediston 2¼, Cookley 3¾'

➡ **page 94**

22 **Ignore** turnings to left and right for 8 km (5 miles), following signs for Harleston and Weybread. At T-j with B1116 L 'Harleston 1'

23 Climb! At T-j with Needham Road R 'Town Centre' to return to the start

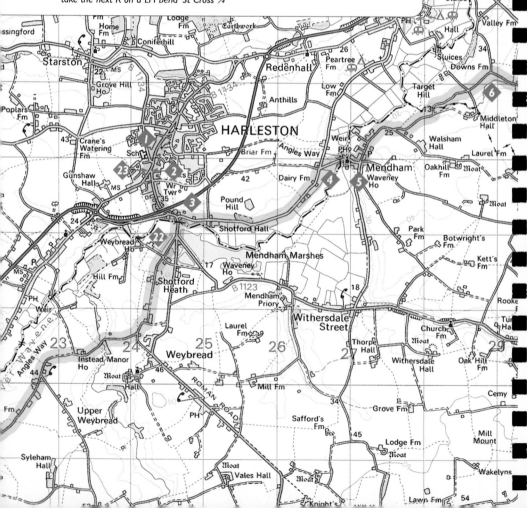

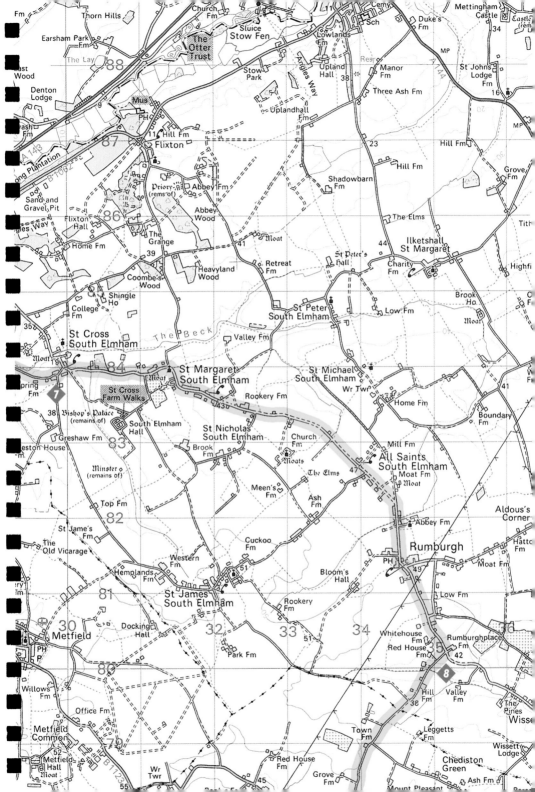

9 After 4 km (2½ miles) at offset X-roads with B1123 R then L 'Cookley 2¼, Huntingfield 2½'

10 **Easy to miss**. After 4¾ km (3 miles) go past the church in Huntingfield. Climb then descend. At the bottom of the hill, just before a small red-brick bridge over river turn R by triangle of grass 'Cratfield 2¾, Laxfield 3'

11 Follow signs for Laxfield for 5¾ km (3½ miles) ignoring turnings to right and left. At T-j with B1117 in Laxfield SA 'Stradbroke 4, Harleston 10'

12 **Ignore** left turn on 'The Link', take the next L by memorial stone 'Brundish 3, Framlingham 7'

13 At T-j with B1116 bear R (in effect SA) 'Stradbroke 4, Fressingfield 5' then shortly after RH bend 1st L 'Brundish 2, Wilby 2'

14 At T-j bear L (in effect SA) 'Horham 3, Worlingworth 4'

➡ page 96

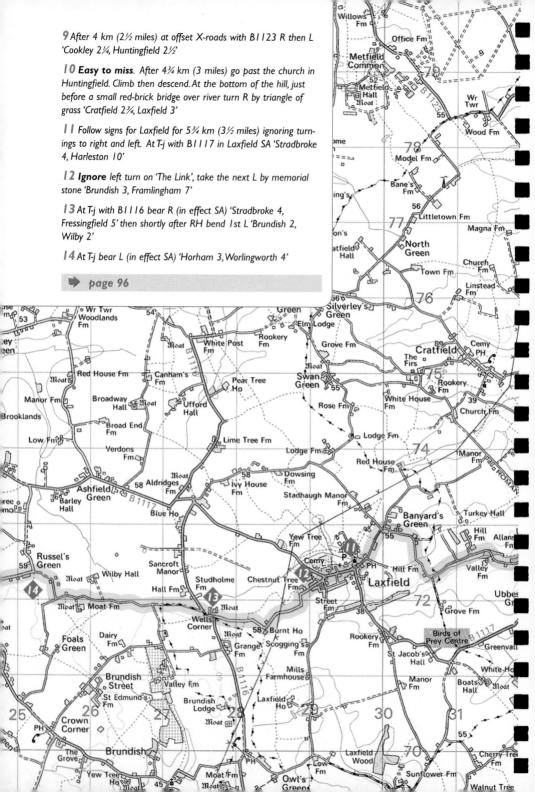

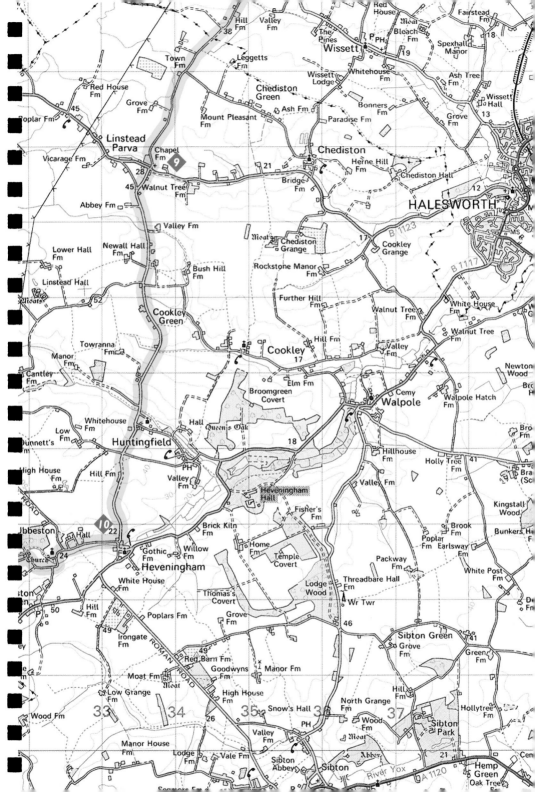

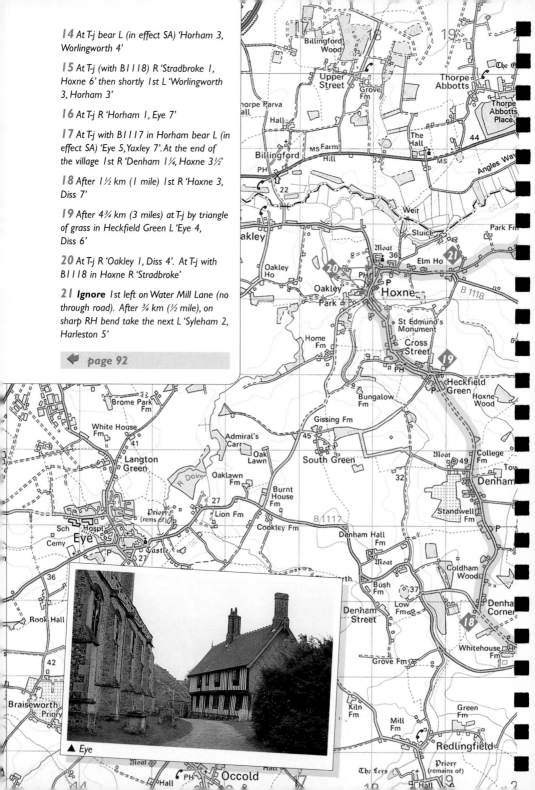

14 At T-j bear L (in effect SA) 'Horham 3, Worlingworth 4'

15 At T-j (with B1118) R 'Stradbroke 1, Hoxne 6' then shortly 1st L 'Worlingworth 3, Horham 3'

16 At T-j R 'Horham 1, Eye 7'

17 At T-j with B1117 in Horham bear L (in effect SA) 'Eye 5, Yaxley 7'. At the end of the village 1st R 'Denham 1¼, Hoxne 3½'

18 After 1½ km (1 mile) 1st R 'Hoxne 3, Diss 7'

19 After 4¾ km (3 miles) at T-j by triangle of grass in Heckfield Green L 'Eye 4, Diss 6'

20 At T-j R 'Oakley 1, Diss 4'. At T-j with B1118 in Hoxne R 'Stradbroke'

21 **Ignore** 1st left on Water Mill Lane (no through road). After ¾ km (½ mile), on sharp RH bend take the next L 'Syleham 2, Harleston 5'

◀ **page 92**

▲ Eye

14 North from Diss to Attleborough

This is one of two rides starting from Diss, an old town lying on the boundary between Norfolk and Suffolk. The boundary at this point, as along so much of its length, is formed by the River Waveney. Throughout East Anglia there are signs of airfields that were built during the Second World War and used by Allied planes in their attacks on German positions. East Anglia was an ideal location: flat, close to the European mainland and out of reach of the V1 and V2 bombs that were directed at London towards the end of the war. This ride passes close to three such airfields. As the demand for aggregate for the construction of motor-ways has increased, many of the airfields have been dug up for their stone and concrete. The ride crosses flat arable land towards the attractive village of Kenninghall with its fine brick and flint walls and pargetting on Church Farm House, a decorative feature frequently seen in Suffolk and Essex. A little fur-ther on, Quidenham's delights include a Viking mound, an unusual round and octagonal church tower, an ornate lodge house to Quidenham Park, and a tea shop at the Post Office. Attleborough's charms are restricted to the small area around the green. A few miles southeast of the town, just south of Carleton Rode, you will come across the extraordinary fairy tale thatch at Fen Farm. The ride turns south and heads across the fertile landscape back to Diss

Start

The Museum in the Market Place, Diss, just off the A143 between Bury St Edmunds and Lowestoft

P Follow signs

Distance and grade

48 km (30 miles)

Easy

Terrain

Undulating arable land. Lowest point – 25m (82 feet) at Quidenham. Highest point – 72m (236 feet) near Carleton Rode

Refreshments:

Lots of choice in **Diss**
Tea shop at PO, **Quidenham**
White Lodge PH, lots of choice in **Attleborough**
Greyhound PH, **Tibenham**

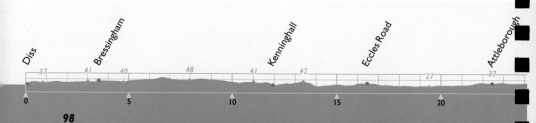

Diss or Attleborough

```
102                 103




100        Diss    101
```

▼ Bressingham Gardens

Places of interest

Diss 1
The town has twisting streets with Tudor, Georgian and Victorian architecture and is busy on Friday market days. The imposing Church of St Mary's dates from the 12th century. The 2½-ha (6-acre) mere is a haven for wildfowl

Bressingham Gardens 1½ km
(1 mile) south of the route at 4
An extensive 210-ha (500-acre) nursery makes an unusual setting for the steam locomotive collection. There are more than 5000 varieties of alpines, heathers, conifers and perennials. The narrow-gauge railway runs across the valley of the River Waveney. There is a splendid Victorian steam roundabout in the museum

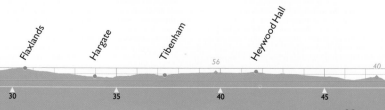

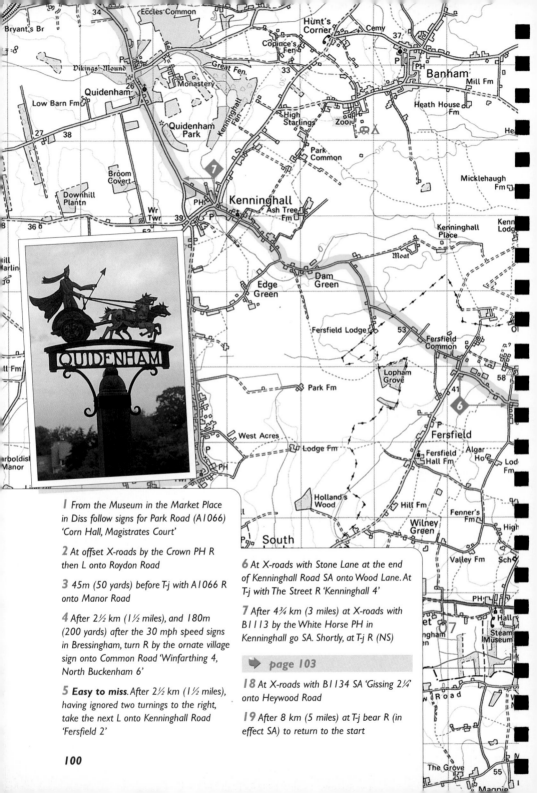

1 From the Museum in the Market Place in Diss follow signs for Park Road (A1066) 'Corn Hall, Magistrates Court'

2 At offset X-roads by the Crown PH R then L onto Roydon Road

3 45m (50 yards) before T-j with A1066 R onto Manor Road

4 After 2½ km (1½ miles), and 180m (200 yards) after the 30 mph speed signs in Bressingham, turn R by the ornate village sign onto Common Road 'Winfarthing 4, North Buckenham 6'

5 **Easy to miss**. After 2½ km (1½ miles), having ignored two turnings to the right, take the next L onto Kenninghall Road 'Fersfield 2'

6 At X-roads with Stone Lane at the end of Kenninghall Road SA onto Wood Lane. At T-j with The Street R 'Kenninghall 4'

7 After 4¾ km (3 miles) at X-roads with B1113 by the White Horse PH in Kenninghall go SA. Shortly, at T-j R (NS)

➡ page 103

18 At X-roads with B1134 SA 'Gissing 2¼' onto Heywood Road

19 After 8 km (5 miles) at T-j bear R (in effect SA) to return to the start

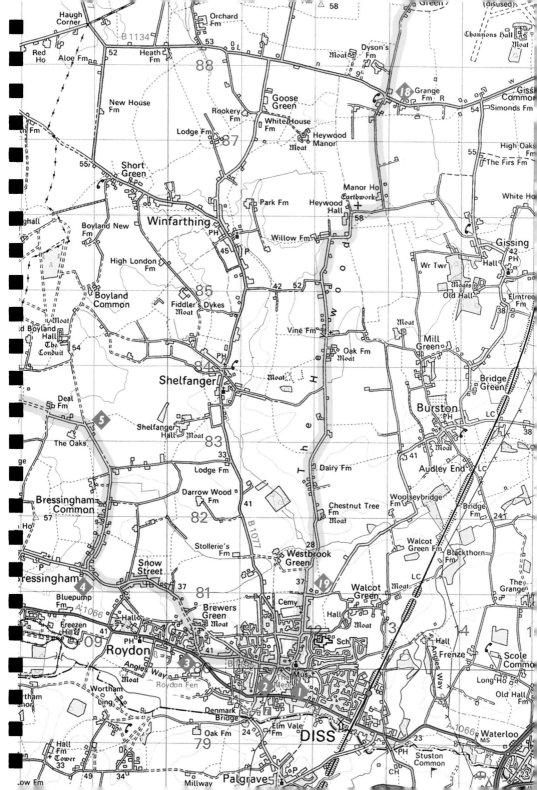

8 Go through Quidenham. After 2½ km (1½ miles), cross railway line. After a further 1½ km (1 mile), at offset X-roads R over bridge then immediately L (NS)

9 After 4¾ km (3 miles) at T-j in Attleborough opposite petrol station R

10 At the end of the one way system, get into the RH lane but go SA onto Besthorpe Road 'Besthorpe 1'

11 At mini-roundabout at the end of humped road R 'Carleton Rode 4, Bunwell 5'

12 At T-j by Give Way sign R 'Carleton Rode 2, Bunwell 3'

13 After 1½ km (1 mile) **ignore** 1st right to New Buckenham, after further 1¼ km (¾ mile) next R at X-roads 'Tibenham 4'

14 At X-roads by triangle of grass at the end of Hall Road SA onto Rode Lane 'New Buckenham 2¾'

15 At offset X-roads with B1113 at the end of Rode Lane R then L onto Ash Lane 'Tibenham 2½'

16 At T-j at the end of Ash Lane R (NS)

17 **Easy to miss.** After 1½ km (1 miles) 1st L onto Mill Road 'Tibenham'

⬅ page 100

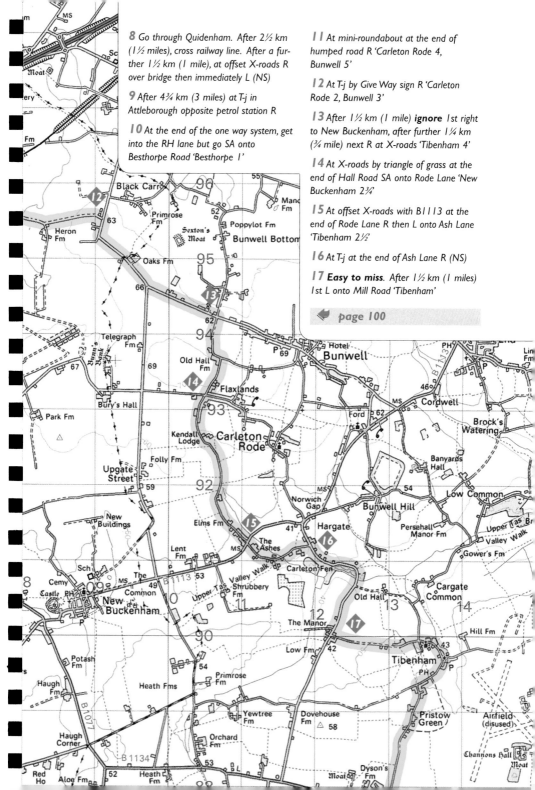

15 West from Diss to Ixworth and the source of the River Waveney

Start

The Museum, Market Place, Diss

P Follow signs

Distance and grade

57 km (35 miles)

Easy

Terrain

Upper Waveney valley, rich arable land with fragments of broadleaf woodland. Lowest point – 20m (66 ft) at the crossing of the River Waveney south of Diss. Highest point – 63 m (206 ft) between Gislingham and Walsham Le Willows

Diss is situated on the Norfolk/Suffolk boundary and this southern ride from the town lies almost entirely within Suffolk. The River Waveney is crossed at Denmark Bridge and the route roughly follows the line of the Norwich–Ipswich railway line. There are thatch and flint houses around the attractive village green at Thrandeston, and soon after crossing the railway line at Mellis there is a straight section across common land which seems out of place in a region so dedicated to intensive agriculture. Another unusual feature appears in Gislingham: a fine large church tower built of red brick – all but a very few of the churches in this part of the world are built of flint. The tour runs onwards and westwards past the timber-framed cottages of Walsham Le Willows to Ixworth with its fine pub, priory ruins and over-hanging houses. The finest architecture of the whole ride lies 3 km (2 miles) north of Ixworth at Bardwell Hall, an immense old house of brick and timber. North and east through Coney Weston and Hopton, the ride drops down to the Waveney valley which you follow all the way back to Diss, passing the thatched houses in Thelnetham and the rough sandy common land close to Roydon.

Nearest railway

Diss

106 Diss 107

108 109

Refreshments:

Lots of choice in **Diss**
Railway Tavern 🍺, **Mellis**
Six Bells PH, **Gislingham**
Blue Boar PH, Six Bells PH,
Walsham Le Willows
Pykkerell PH 🍺🍺*, Greyhound PH,* **Ixworth**
Six Bells PH 🍺🍺*, Dun Cow PH,* **Bardwell**
White Horse PH 🍺*,* **Thelnetham**

Places of interest

Walsham Le Willows 10
A village set in the heart of parkland, with timber-framed cottages and a fine confusion of eaves and roof levels. The Six Bells Inn derives its name from the church tower

Ixworth 12
A small village with a grand abbey converted to a dwelling house in the 16th century. It was started in the 12th century and rebuilt over the following centuries

▼Diss

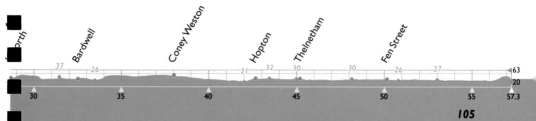

orth   Bardwell   Coney Weston   Hopton   Thelnetham   Fen Street

37   26   21   32   30   30   26   27   63
                                                      20
30   35   40   45   50   55   57.3

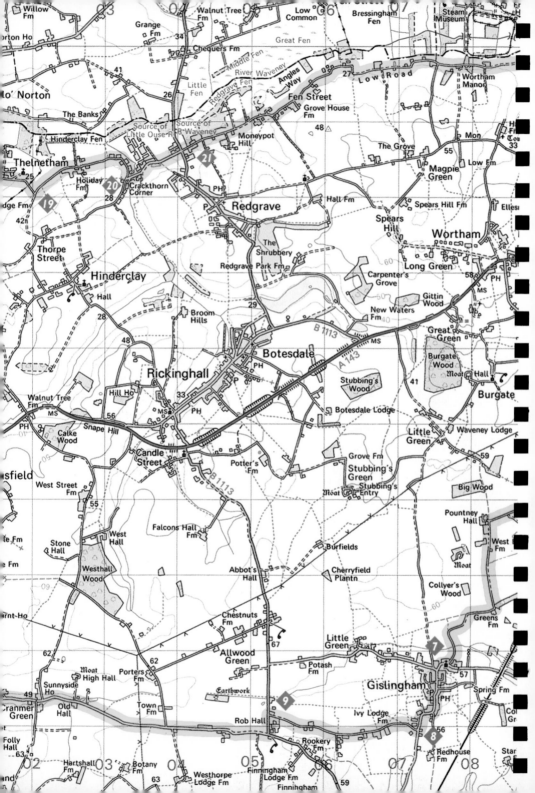

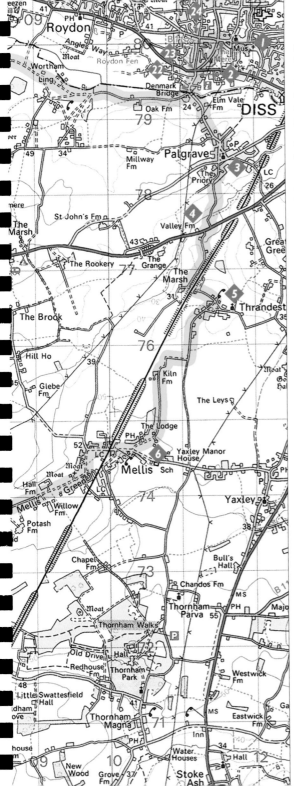

1 *From the Museum in the Market Place in Diss follow signs for Park Road (A1066) 'Corn Hall, Magistrates Court'*

2 *At T-j at the end of St Nicholas Street by the Crown PH turn L 'Thetford, Norwich, Great Yarmouth'. At T-j with A1066 R then L onto Denmark Street*

3 **Busy section**. *Cross into Suffolk. At X-roads SA onto Priory Road 'Thrandeston 1¼, Mellis 3¼'*

4 *At offset X-roads with (new) A143 R then L 'Thrandeston, Little Green'*

5 *Shortly after the start of Thrandeston 1st R by the village green and telephone box 'Mellis 2'*

6 *At T-j with Yaxley Road in Mellis R 'Wortham 2½'. **Ignore** 1st left to Thornham. Cross railway line and take next L 'Gislingham 3, Finningham 4'*

7 *After 4¾ km (3 miles) at T-j in Gislingham R 'Finningham 2, Rickinghall 4'*

8 *Shortly after the end of Gislingham, 1st R onto Back Street 'Walsham 5'*

9 *At T-j with B1113 at the end of Ball Street L 'Finningham 1, Stowmarket 8' then 1st R 'Walsham 3'*

➡ **page 108**

19 *On sharp RH bend ¾ km (½ mile) after the end of Thelnetham L onto Fen Road 'Redgrave, Diss 6'*

20 *At T-j by triangle of grass L 'Redgrave, Diss 6'*

21 *At X-roads (with B1113) by Give Way sign SA onto Fen Street 'Palgrave 5, Diss 5'*

22 *Follow for 8 km (5 miles). At T-j by bridge L 'Diss ½, Roydon 1'*

23 *At X-roads with A1066 SA onto Croft Lane 'Unsuitable for HGVs'*

24 *At X-roads by Give Way sign R onto Roydon Road. At offset X-roads R then L onto St Nicholas Street to return to the start*

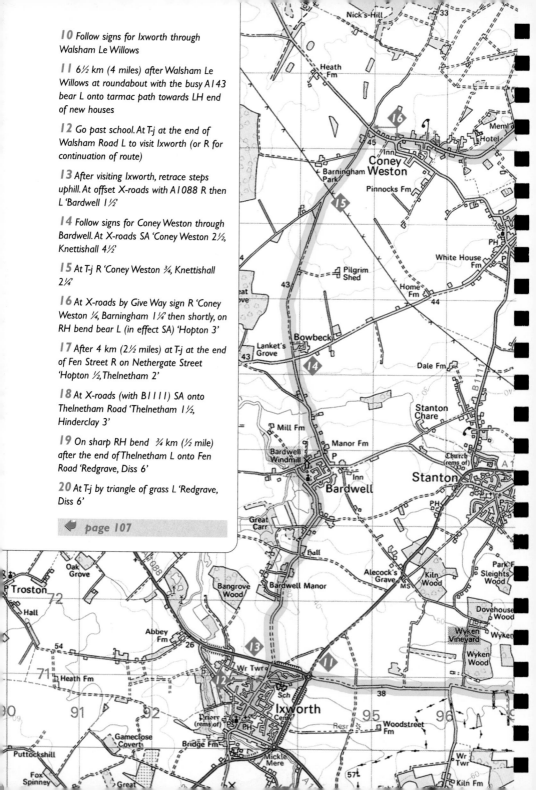

10 Follow signs for Ixworth through Walsham Le Willows

11 6½ km (4 miles) after Walsham Le Willows at roundabout with the busy A143 bear L onto tarmac path towards LH end of new houses

12 Go past school. At T-j at the end of Walsham Road L to visit Ixworth (or R for continuation of route)

13 After visiting Ixworth, retrace steps uphill. At offset X-roads with A1088 R then L 'Bardwell 1½'

14 Follow signs for Coney Weston through Bardwell. At X-roads SA 'Coney Weston 2½, Knettishall 4½'

15 At T-j R 'Coney Weston ¾, Knettishall 2¼'

16 At X-roads by Give Way sign R 'Coney Weston ¼, Barningham 1¼' then shortly, on RH bend bear L (in effect SA) 'Hopton 3'

17 After 4 km (2½ miles) at T-j at the end of Fen Street R on Nethergate Street 'Hopton ½, Thelnetham 2'

18 At X-roads (with B1111) SA onto Thelnetham Road 'Thelnetham 1½, Hinderclay 3'

19 On sharp RH bend ¾ km (½ mile) after the end of Thelnetham L onto Fen Road 'Redgrave, Diss 6'

20 At T-j by triangle of grass L 'Redgrave, Diss 6'

◀ **page 107**

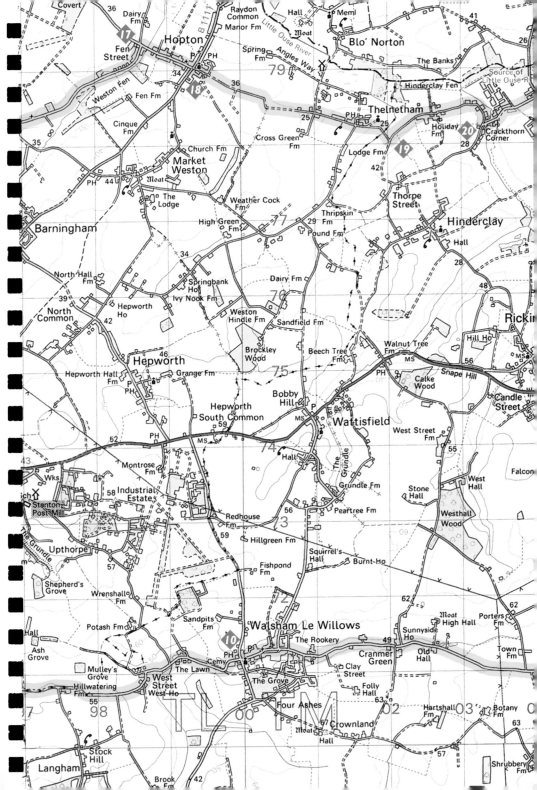

Through the heart of Fenland from Ely to Chatteris

Start

The Lamb Inn, near the cathedral in Ely

P Follow signs

Distance and grade

67 km (42 miles)

Easy

Terrain

Almost all near sea level: the flattest ride in a flat region!

Nearest railway

Ely

Compared to most of Great Britain, East Anglia is flat: to the east of the A1 the land rarely rises above 150m (500 ft). The northern half of East Anglia (the area covered by this book) is even flatter, rarely rising above 90m (300 ft). This ride from Ely runs across the dark soil of the fens, some of the richest and most productive agricultural land in the whole of Britain. Ely Cathedral soars above the surrounding Fenland, its scale dwarfing all around it. The limited crossings of the Wash or the Old Bedford River dictate the shape of this ride: the bridge over the river at Welney is the only road crossing for 27km (17 miles) between Mepal in the southwest and Downham Market in the northeast. The ride heads west to Coveney, passing between the rich, dark fields surrounded by drainage ditches. Remember to look behind you to see the silhouette of Ely Cathedral. The houses are almost all brick-built: there is a particularly fine old red-brick house in Witcham. Sutton offers little to detain the cyclist, but just beyond the village, the pub at Sutton Gault with its garden over-looking the river makes a fine break. Chatteris has a few old buildings in its centre, but this is above all a ride through the dark fenland and for the rest of its course it passes through nowhere bigger than the villages of Manea ('Maynee') and Little Downham, by which time you are being drawn back again to the looming shape of Ely Cathedral.

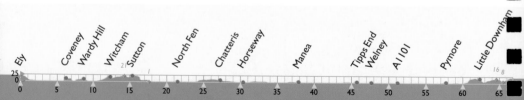

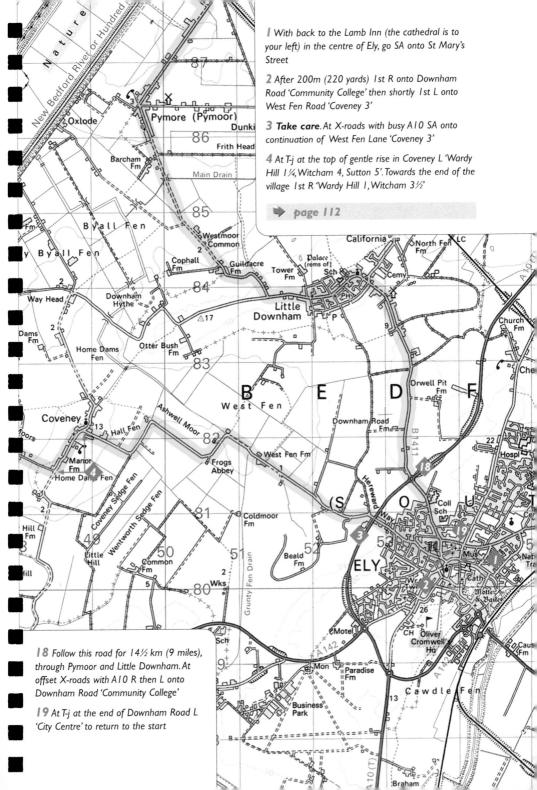

1 With back to the Lamb Inn (the cathedral is to your left) in the centre of Ely, go SA onto St Mary's Street

2 After 200m (220 yards) 1st R onto Downham Road 'Community College' then shortly 1st L onto West Fen Road 'Coveney 3'

3 *Take care*. At X-roads with busy A10 SA onto continuation of West Fen Lane 'Coveney 3'

4 At T-j at the top of gentle rise in Coveney L 'Wardy Hill 1¼, Witcham 4, Sutton 5'. Towards the end of the village 1st R 'Wardy Hill 1, Witcham 3½'

➡ page 112

18 Follow this road for 14½ km (9 miles), through Pymoor and Little Downham. At offset X-roads with A10 R then L onto Downham Road 'Community College'

19 At T-j at the end of Downham Road L 'City Centre' to return to the start

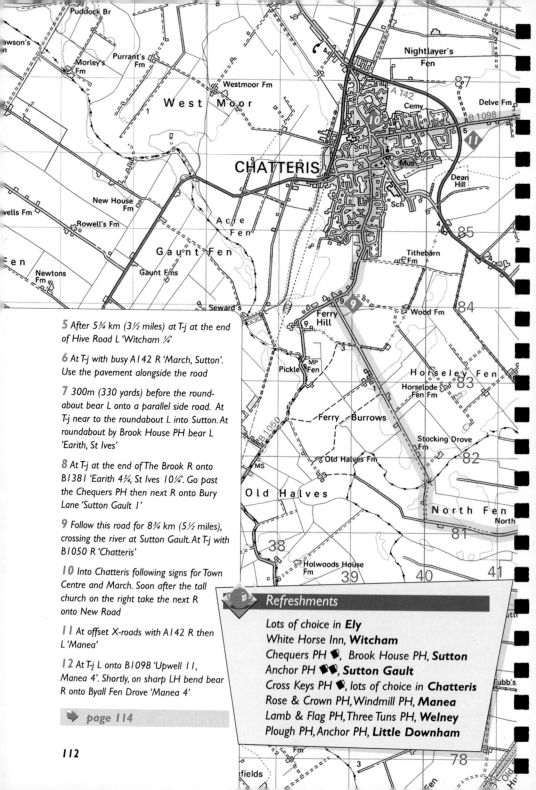

5 After 5¾ km (3½ miles) at T-j at the end of Hive Road L 'Witcham ¼'

6 At T-j with busy A142 R 'March, Sutton'. Use the pavement alongside the road

7 300m (330 yards) before the round-about bear L onto a parallel side road. At T-j near to the roundabout L into Sutton. At roundabout by Brook House PH bear L 'Earith, St Ives'

8 At T-j at the end of The Brook R onto B1381 'Earith 4¾, St Ives 10¼'. Go past the Chequers PH then next R onto Bury Lane 'Sutton Gault 1'

9 Follow this road for 8¾ km (5½ miles), crossing the river at Sutton Gault. At T-j with B1050 R 'Chatteris'

10 Into Chatteris following signs for Town Centre and March. Soon after the tall church on the right take the next R onto New Road

11 At offset X-roads with A142 R then L 'Manea'

12 At T-j L onto B1098 'Upwell 11, Manea 4'. Shortly, on sharp LH bend bear R onto Byall Fen Drove 'Manea 4'

➡ **page 114**

Refreshments

Lots of choice in **Ely**
White Horse Inn, **Witcham**
Chequers PH 🍴, Brook House PH, **Sutton**
Anchor PH 🍴🍴, **Sutton Gault**
Cross Keys PH 🍴, lots of choice in **Chatteris**
Rose & Crown PH, Windmill PH, **Manea**
Lamb & Flag PH, Three Tuns PH, **Welney**
Plough PH, Anchor PH, **Little Downham**

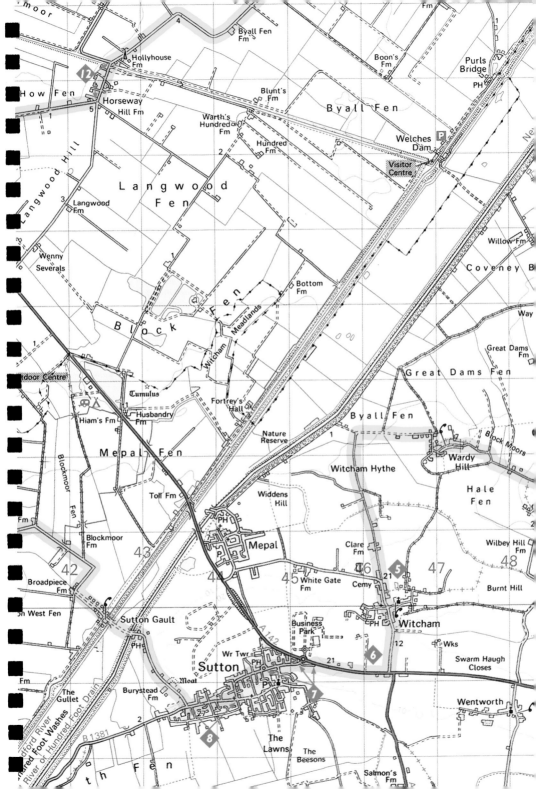

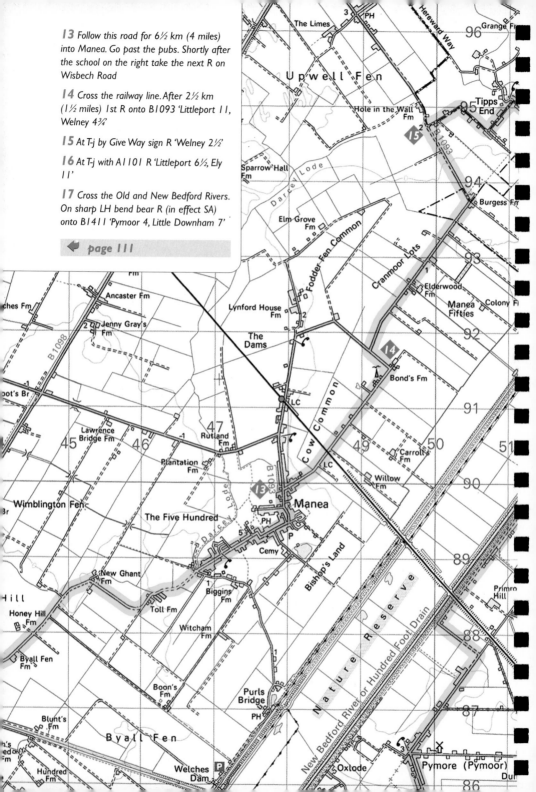

13 *Follow this road for 6½ km (4 miles) into Manea. Go past the pubs. Shortly after the school on the right take the next R on Wisbech Road*

14 *Cross the railway line. After 2½ km (1½ miles) 1st R onto B1093 'Littleport 11, Welney 4¾'*

15 *At T-j by Give Way sign R 'Welney 2½'*

16 *At T-j with A1101 R 'Littleport 6½, Ely 11'*

17 *Cross the Old and New Bedford Rivers. On sharp LH bend bear R (in effect SA) onto B1411 'Pymoor 4, Little Downham 7'*

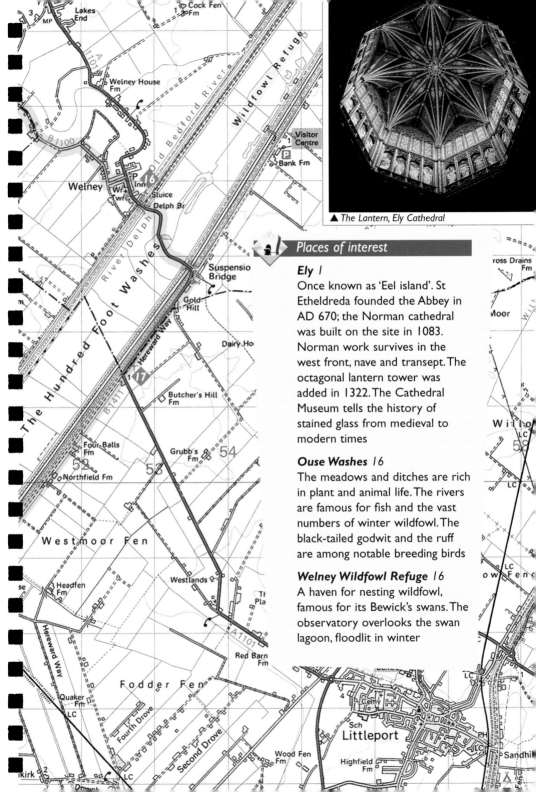

▲ The Lantern, Ely Cathedral

Places of interest

Ely 1
Once known as 'Eel island'. St Etheldreda founded the Abbey in AD 670; the Norman cathedral was built on the site in 1083. Norman work survives in the west front, nave and transept. The octagonal lantern tower was added in 1322. The Cathedral Museum tells the history of stained glass from medieval to modern times

Ouse Washes 16
The meadows and ditches are rich in plant and animal life. The rivers are famous for fish and the vast numbers of winter wildfowl. The black-tailed godwit and the ruff are among notable breeding birds

Welney Wildfowl Refuge 16
A haven for nesting wildfowl, famous for its Bewick's swans. The observatory overlooks the swan lagoon, floodlit in winter

Along the Peddars Way from Castle Acre to Holme next the Sea (the northern half)

The Peddars Way was built by the Romans in the second half of the first century AD and provides one of the finest off-road routes in all of East Anglia. The ride has been split into two sections, described in off-road routes 1 and 2, each of which should be manageable in a day. However, as the ride is a linear, there-and-back route, it is possible to do as much or as little as you like. The best option of all might be to have somebody drop you at the start near to Thetford and pick you up at the end when you reach the sea at Holme. The ride described here starts at the halfway point of Castle Acre, a delightful village of brick and flint which is an excellent base for both on-road and off-road rides. The ride is a mixture of lanes and tracks – some of the latter are likely to be hard going (ie muddy) from late autumn to late spring. There is more tarmac at the start of the ride near to Castle Acre but the lanes carry very little

Start

The Ostrich PH, Castle Acre, north of Swaffham

🅿 In the square or by the castle ruins in Castle Acre

Distance and grade

39 km (24 miles) one way

Moderate. Avoid late autumn to late spring when the tracks are very muddy

Terrain

Mixture of quiet lanes and mainly stone-based tracks over undulating arable land with some broadleaf woodland. Sea views at the northern end of the ride. Lowest point – sea level at Holme next the Sea. Highest point – 95 m (312 ft) at several points during the first third of the ride

! The most important instructions on the way north are 11–12 near Fring and 16–17 close to the coast.

Nearest railway

King's Lynn, 17km
(11 miles) west of the
route near to Great
Massingham

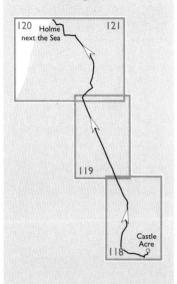

traffic and are a delight in themselves, passing through broadleaf woodland. The course of the Peddars Way bridle route and footpath run together, straight as an arrow for several miles in a generally northwesterly direction as far as Fring where the two routes diverge, rejoining in Holme next the Sea. The sea finally comes into view at the crest of the last hill before the coast, some 6 miles north of Fring. From here there is a steady downhill ride out to the dunes on the coast

Refreshments

Ostrich PH 🍴🍴, Albert Victor PH,
tearooms, **Castle Acre**
White Horse PH, **Holme next the Sea**
Pubs just off the route in:
**Great Massingham, Harpley 🍴, Great
Bircham 🍴, Docking 🍴, Sedgeford 🍴,
Ringstead 🍴🍴**

Places of interest

Great Bircham Windmill 2 miles west of 11
Norfolk's finest working corn mill stands on a site dating
back to the 1700s. A five-floor climb reveals the mill
machinery and sails. There is a shop, tearoom and bakery

Castle Acre 1
See page 37

Fring

Summerfield

Holme next the Sea

59   70 60   25   42   95

20   25   30   35   38.9

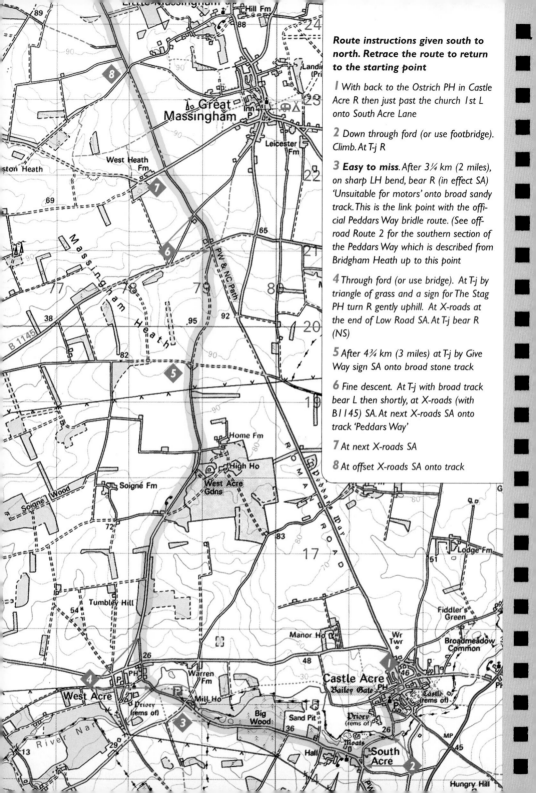

Route instructions given south to north. Retrace the route to return to the starting point

1 With back to the Ostrich PH in Castle Acre R then just past the church 1st L onto South Acre Lane

2 Down through ford (or use footbridge). Climb. At T-j R

3 **Easy to miss.** After 3¼ km (2 miles), on sharp LH bend, bear R (in effect SA) 'Unsuitable for motors' onto broad sandy track. This is the link point with the official Peddars Way bridle route. (See off-road Route 2 for the southern section of the Peddars Way which is described from Bridgham Heath up to this point

4 Through ford (or use bridge). At T-j by triangle of grass and a sign for The Stag PH turn R gently uphill. At X-roads at the end of Low Road SA. At T-j bear R (NS)

5 After 4¾ km (3 miles) at T-j by Give Way sign SA onto broad stone track

6 Fine descent. At T-j with broad track bear L then shortly, at X-roads (with B1145) SA. At next X-roads SA onto track 'Peddars Way'

7 At next X-roads SA

8 At offset X-roads SA onto track

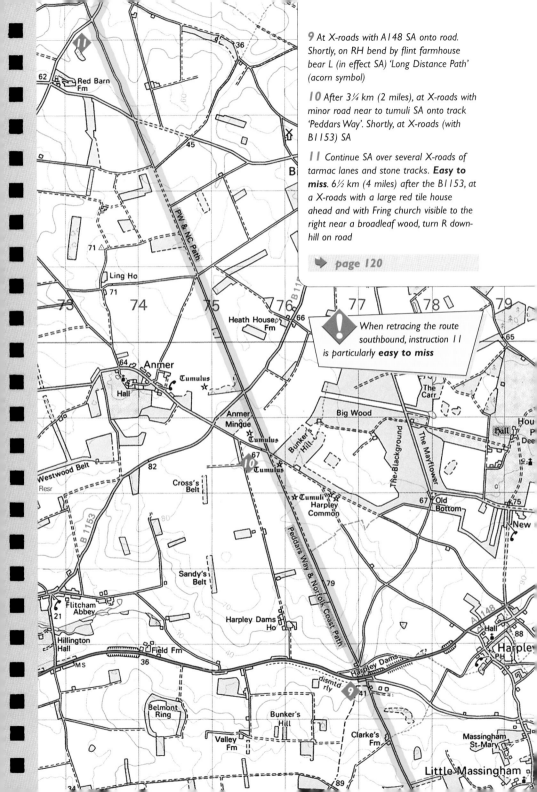

9 At X-roads with A148 SA onto road. Shortly, on RH bend by flint farmhouse bear L (in effect SA) 'Long Distance Path' (acorn symbol)

10 After 3¼ km (2 miles), at X-roads with minor road near to tumuli SA onto track 'Peddars Way'. Shortly, at X-roads (with B1153) SA

11 Continue SA over several X-roads of tarmac lanes and stone tracks. **Easy to miss.** 6½ km (4 miles) after the B1153, at a X-roads with a large red tile house ahead and with Fring church visible to the right near a broadleaf wood, turn R downhill on road

➡ **page 120**

When retracing the route southbound, instruction 11 is particularly **easy to miss**

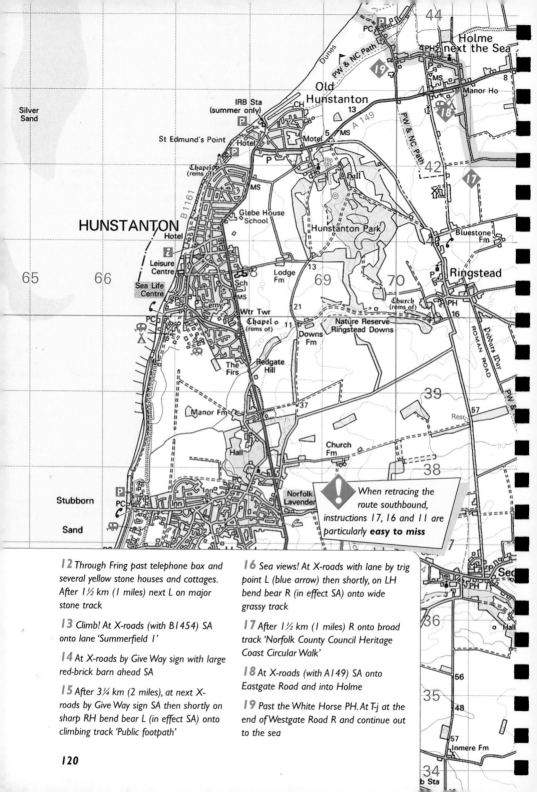

When retracing the route southbound, instructions 17, 16 and 11 are particularly **easy to miss**

12 Through Fring past telephone box and several yellow stone houses and cottages. After 1½ km (1 miles) next L on major stone track

13 Climb! At X-roads (with B1454) SA onto lane 'Summerfield 1'

14 At X-roads by Give Way sign with large red-brick barn ahead SA

15 After 3¼ km (2 miles), at next X-roads by Give Way sign SA then shortly on sharp RH bend bear L (in effect SA) onto climbing track 'Public footpath'

16 Sea views! At X-roads with lane by trig point L (blue arrow) then shortly, on LH bend bear R (in effect SA) onto wide grassy track

17 After 1½ km (1 miles) R onto broad track 'Norfolk County Council Heritage Coast Circular Walk'

18 At X-roads (with A149) SA onto Eastgate Road and into Holme

19 Past the White Horse PH. At T-j at the end of Westgate Road R and continue out to the sea

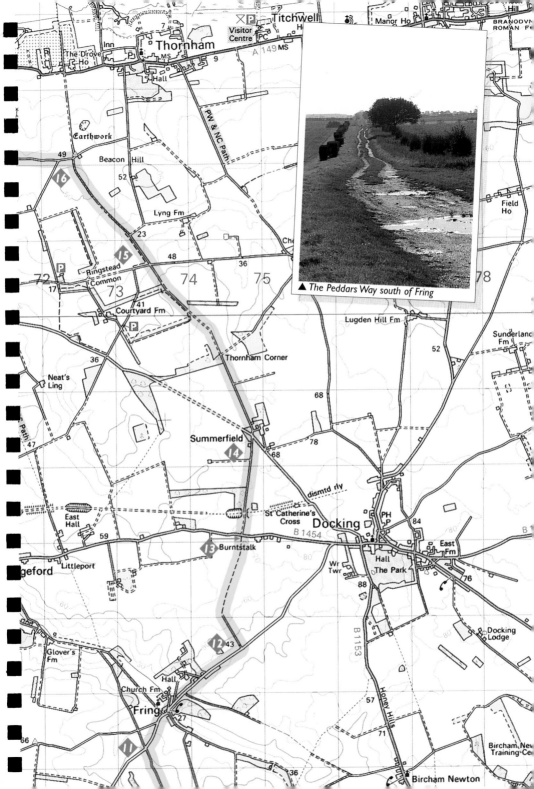

Thornham

Titchwell

Manor Ho

BRANODVN
ROMAN F

Visitor
Centre

PC

A 149 MS

The Drove
Ho

Inn

MS

9

Hall

PW & NC Path

Earthwork

Field
Ho

49

Beacon Hill

16

52

Lyng Fm

23

15

48

36

Che

72

P

Ringstead
Common

73

74

75

78

17

41

Courtyard Fm

P

Lugden Hill Fm

Sunderland
Fm

Thornham Corner

52

36

Neat's
Ling

68

47

Path

78

Summerfield

14

68

dismtd rly

East
Hall

St Catherine's
Cross

Docking

PH
P

84

59

13

Burntstalk

B 1454

East
Fm

geford

Littleport

80

Wr
Twr

Hall
The Park

B1

76

88

Docking
Lodge

12

43

B 1153

80

Glover's
Fm

Honey Hills

57

Hall

Church Fm

71

Fring

27

Bircham New
Training Ce

11

66

36

Bircham Newton

▲ The Peddars Way south of Fring

2

Peddars Way from Bridgham Heath to Castle Acre (the southern half)

This ride describes the southern half of the Peddars Way (the northern half is covered in off-road ride 1). It is also a linear, there-and-back ride, overall sandier, more wooded and slightly less undulating than the northern half. The starting point is not particularly auspicious – a track lying just north of a fast section of dual carriageway on the A11. The route passes through a sandy heathland of pines, silver birch and fern that is not unlike parts of Surrey. There are frequent Ministry of Defence signs indicating that the area is used for training. From South Pickenham the route turns west towards the Iceni Village at Cockley Cley before skirting round Swaffham towards the valley of the River Nar. After a fast descent to the river you have a choice of leaving the Peddars Way to discover the delights of Castle Acre or of continuing northwards along the line of the long distance path as it heads towards the sea at Holme.

Start

Just off the A11, 8 km (5 miles) northeast of Thetford, at National Grid reference TL934871. Proceeding northeast from Thetford on the A1075 / A11 the route starts on a track 1½ km (1 mile) after the start of the A11 dual carriageway next to signs which read 'Danger. MOD Range' '68' and 'Peddars Way'

P At start

Distance and grade

46 km (29 miles) one way

Moderate

Terrain

Quiet lanes and tracks. Lowest point – 21m (69 ft) at the crossing of the River Nar near to Castle Acre. Highest point – 78m (255 ft) just to the south of the Nar valley near Castle Acre

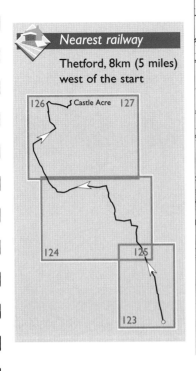

Nearest railway

Thetford, 8km (5 miles) west of the start

Route instructions given south to north. Retrace the route to return to the starting point

1 From the layby just off the A11, 8 km (5 miles) northeast of Thetford, at National Grid reference TL934871, follow Peddars Way signs along the tarmac lane northwards away from the A11. Cross the railway line. Tarmac turns to gravel then rougher track. Keep following Peddars Way signs

2 After 3¼ km (2 miles), at X-roads with road SA 'Long Distance Path'. Follow track between the brick supports of the old railway bridge then bear R. At T-j with main road (A1075) R then shortly after the Dog & Partridge PH 1st road L 'Peddars Way'

3 After 2 km (1¼ miles), shortly after a road joins from the right by triangle of grass take the next track R 'Spanta access'

4 Ignore right turn to Watering Farm. At X-roads with tarmac ('Army / Danger' signs to the left) SA betwen large concrete blocks [**Or** turn R here for the Chequers PH in Thompson]

5 At two more X-roads with tarmac SA onto continuation of track

 page 124

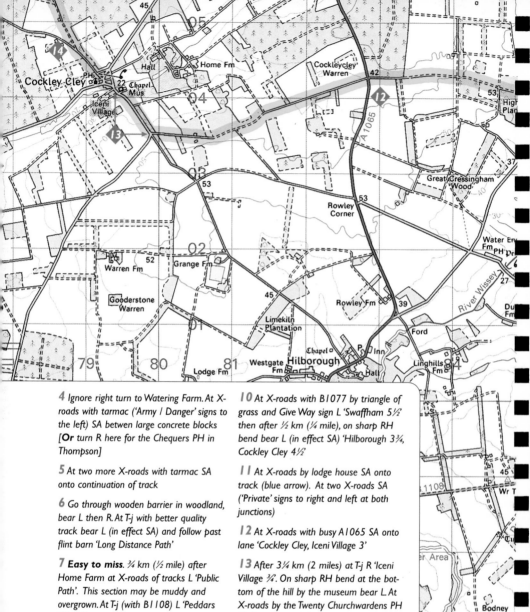

4 Ignore right turn to Watering Farm. At X-roads with tarmac ('Army / Danger' signs to the left) SA betwen large concrete blocks [**Or** turn R here for the Chequers PH in Thompson]

5 At two more X-roads with tarmac SA onto continuation of track

6 Go through wooden barrier in woodland, bear L then R. At T-j with better quality track bear L (in effect SA) and follow past flint barn 'Long Distance Path'

7 **Easy to miss.** ¾ km (½ mile) after Home Farm at X-roads of tracks L 'Public Path'. This section may be muddy and overgrown. At T-j (with B1108) L 'Peddars Way'. Busy section

8 After 2 km (1¼ miles), having ignored 1st right at minor X-roads ('Byroad'), take the 2nd road to the R 'Little Cressingham' then shortly, at X-roads by the White Horse PH R 'South Pickenham 2½'

9 At X-roads by Give Way sign SA 'Peddars Way'

10 At X-roads with B1077 by triangle of grass and Give Way sign L 'Swaffham 5½' then after ½ km (¼ mile), on sharp RH bend bear L (in effect SA) 'Hilborough 3¾, Cockley Cley 4½'

11 At X-roads by lodge house SA onto track (blue arrow). At two X-roads SA ('Private' signs to right and left at both junctions)

12 At X-roads with busy A1065 SA onto lane 'Cockley Cley, Iceni Village 3'

13 After 3¼ km (2 miles) at T-j R 'Iceni Village ¾'. On sharp RH bend at the bottom of the hill by the museum bear L. At X-roads by the Twenty Churchwardens PH SA 'Beachamwell 2½'

14 ¾ km (½ mile) after the end of the village 1st major track to the R into woodland 'Bridleway'

➡ page 127

When retracing the route southbound, instructions 7 and 6 are particularly **easy to miss**

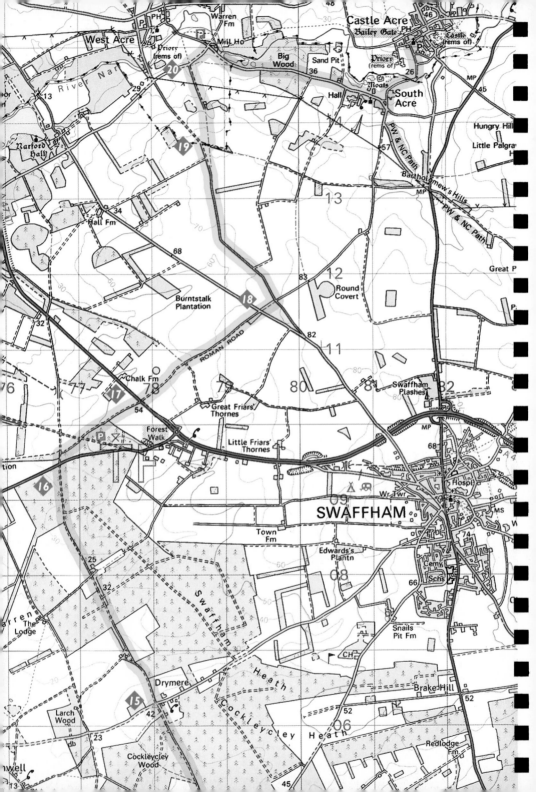

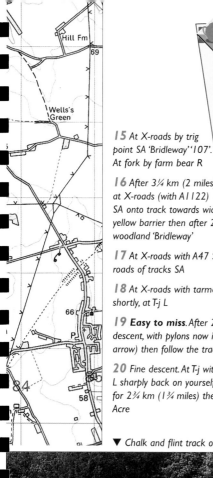

Refreshments

Dog & Partridge PH, **Wretham**

Chequers PH 🍴🍴, **Thompson** (1½ miles east of the route at 4)

White Horse PH, **Little Cressingham**

Windmill PH 🍴, **Great Cressingham** (2 miles west of the route at 9)

Twenty Churchwardens PH 🍴, **Cockley Cley**

Lots of choice in **Swaffham**

Ostrich PH 🍴🍴, **Albert Victor PH**, tearooms, **Castle Acre**

15 At X-roads by trig point SA 'Bridleway' '107'. At fork by farm bear R

16 After 3¼ km (2 miles) at X-roads (with A1122) SA onto track towards wide yellow barrier then after 200 yards turn R alongside edge of woodland 'Bridleway'

17 At X-roads with A47 SA 'Fincham Drove. Bridleway'. At X-roads of tracks SA

18 At X-roads with tarmac SA (blue arrow) then shortly, at T-j L

19 **Easy to miss.** After 2½ km (1½ miles), on gentle descent, with pylons now in sight, turn R onto track (blue arrow) then follow the track round to the L

> **!** When retracing the route southbound, instructions 20 and 18 are particularly **easy to miss**

20 Fine descent. At T-j with road R then after ½ km (¼ mile) 1st L sharply back on yourself for continuation of Peddars Way **or** SA for 2¾ km (1¾ miles) then 1st L after the church 'Ford' for Castle Acre

▼ Chalk and flint track on the Peddars Way south of Little Cressingham

From Reepham to North Walsham along the Marriotts Way and Weavers Way

Start

The old railway station at Reepham, 20 km (12 miles) northwest of Norwich

P As above. The entrance to the Old Railway Station is 1¼ km (¾ mile) north of the crossroads in the centre of Reepham on the B1145 towards Aylsham (opposite the Crown PH)

Distance and grade

21 km (13 miles) one way

 Moderate

Terrain

Dismantled railway path with mixture of embankments and cuttings with rich variety of wildflowers. No hills. The surface varies but should be passable to hybrid and mountain bikes

It is possible to create a 30-mile one-way ride by connecting the Weavers Way with the Marriotts Way and linking Norwich to North Walsham via Drayton, Lenwade, Reepham and Aylsham, this representing one of the longest recreational railway path rides in the country. So often the disused railways have been sold off piecemeal to adjacent landowners. By luck, this one was running until as recently as 1985 and so has not suffered in the same way. The attractive town of Aylsham is the link between the two separate paths: it is explored on the outward leg, the return trip using an off-road link skirting the north of the town. The quality of the surface varies: on the Marriotts Way, between Reepham and Aylsham, a narrow section has been improved with compacted aggregate, although it is rarely wide enough to ride two abreast. Beyond Aylsham the surface is slightly rougher but not segregated into horse and bike sections. There is a wide variety of wildflowers along both paths. A second, circular ride is possible from Reepham using the Themelthorpe Loop and the signposted shortcut forming an enjoyable 11-km (7-mile) trip (see off-road route 4).

Reepham   41   39   Cawston   30   32

0   5   10

Nearest railway

North Walsham

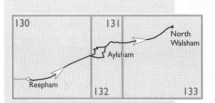

130
131
North Walsham
Aylsham
Reepham
132
133

Places of interest

Reepham 1

An 18th-century market town with Georgian houses and half-timbered dwellings, where three churches used to share a single churchyard. Two remain – they are linked by the choir vestry. One has been a ruin since 1543. There is a sundial over the door of the Georgian Old Brewery

Aylsham 2–3

A market town with splendid old buildings: the Manor House and Abbots Hall date from the early 1600s and the Old Hall from 1689. The rose-covered grave of the landscape gardener Humphry Repton lies in the churchyard of the 14th-century St Michael's Church

Refreshments:

Kings Arms PH 🍺, Old Brewery House PH 🍺, lots of choice in **Reepham**
Refreshments just off the route in **Cawston**
Greens PH 🍺, lots of choice in **Aylsham**
Bluebell PH 🍺, lots of choice in
North Walsham

Blickling Hall 1 mile north of 13
See page 43

▼ Blickling Hall

1 From the Reepham Station car park descend to the railway line and turn R (east)

2 At T-j (with B1354) opposite the Bure Valley Railway Station in Aylsham turn L. Follow road round to the L then take next R through Market Square towards Town Hall

3 At T-j L 'Ingworth' then 1st R onto White Hart Street 'Tuttington. Bypass'

4 Past the Stonemasons Arms PH. Cross the river then 1st L onto one way street. Cross railway bridge, 1st R onto Banningham Road, then 1st L onto continuation of Banningham Road 'Weavers Way'

5 **Ignore** 1st right (no through road). Take next R onto track at X-roads with 'No through road' sign ahead. At X-roads with busy A140 SA onto track. This section may be rough

6 At T-j with a better, stone-based track R then L to join the dismantled railway line. Follow for 6½ km (4 miles)

➡️ **page 132**

10 At the end of the dismantled railway track, with a house ahead, R then 1st track L 'No through road'. Rough section

11 At T-j with the busy A140 SA onto track. At cross-roads with tarmac L

12 At T-j at the end of Banningham Road sharp R (ie not the main road). After 50 yards L into gravel car park then R onto railway path. Follow for 1¼ km (¾ mile)

13 At T-j (with the B1354) SA. Short, steep climb. At T-j with tarmac path L and follow this parallel to the road

14 **Easy to miss.** Opposite handsome red-brick house turn R 'Weavers Way' through gap in fence just beyond stile then R through bridlegate. Follow grassy track through the long narrow field opposite the house

15 Just before the end of the field bear L through bridlegate. At T-j with the road L then 1st track R by a red-brick house

16 At start of tarmac, as lane swings L, bear R (in effect SA) 'Marriotts Way / Weavers Way Link'. At T-j with road L then immediately R onto Marriotts Way to rejoin outward route for 8 km (5 miles) back to Reepham

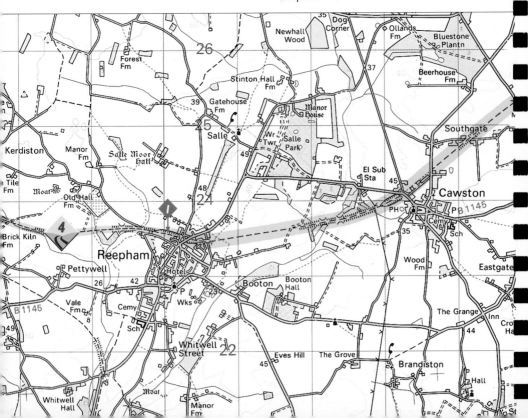

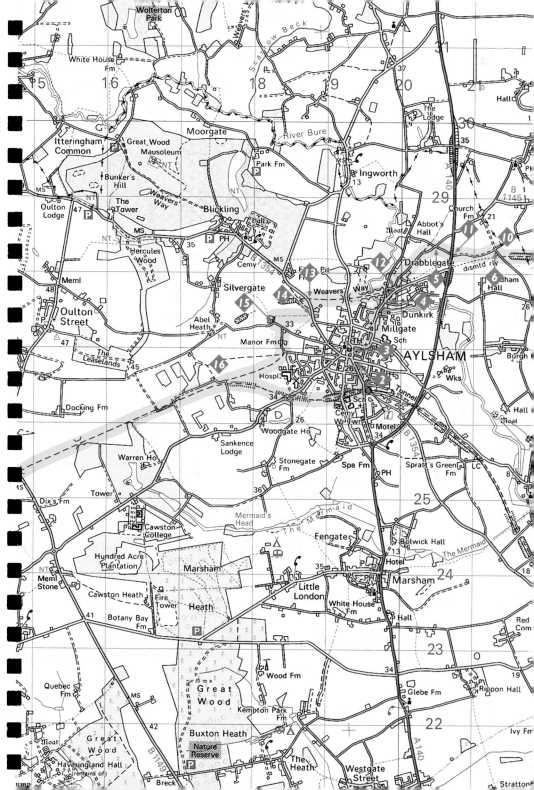

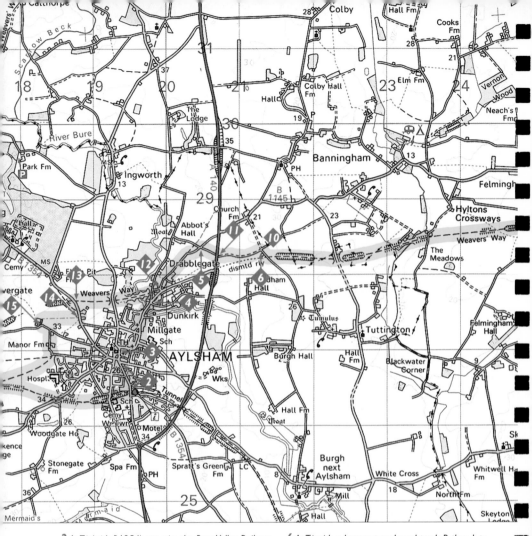

2 At T-j (with B1354) opposite the Bure Valley Railway Station in Aylsham turn L. Follow road round to the L then take next R through Market Square towards Town Hall

3 At T-j L 'Ingworth' then 1st R onto White Hart Street 'Tuttington. Bypass'

4 Past the Stonemasons Arms PH. Cross the river then 1st L onto one way street. Cross railway bridge, 1st R onto Banningham Road, then 1st L onto continuation of Banningham Road 'Weavers Way'

5 **Ignore** 1st right (no through road). Take next R onto track at X-roads with 'No through road' sign ahead. At X-roads with busy A140 SA onto track. This section may be rough

6 At T-j with a better, stone-based track R then L to join the dismantled railway line. Follow for 6½ km (4 miles)

7 On the outskirts of North Walsham, at X-roads with Station Road at the end of the railway path SA onto lane opposite. At T-j R under railway bridge and follow the one way system around to the R to the Market Cross in the centre of North Walsham

8 From the Market Cross in North Walsham take Kings Arms Street past the Kings Arms Hotel sign-posted 'A149, B1150'. At the end of the road turn R then stay in the LH lane, following signs for Aylsham

▲ Weavers' Way near North Walsham

9 Immediately after passing beneath the road and railway bridges turn L (NS). At T-j (with Station Road) SA onto track 'Weavers Way'. Follow for 6½ km (4 miles)

10 At the end of the dismantled railway track, with a house ahead, R then 1st track L 'No through road'. Rough section

11 At T-j with the busy A140 SA onto track. At crossroads with tarmac L

12 At T-j at the end of Banningham Road sharp R (ie not the main road). After 45m (50 yards) L into gravel car park then R onto railway path. Follow for 1¼ km (¾ mile)

13 At T-j (with the B1354) SA. Short, steep climb. At T-j with tarmac path L and follow this parallel to the road

14 **Easy to miss**. Opposite handsome red-brick house turn R 'Weavers Way' through gap in fence just beyond stile then R through bridlegate. Follow grassy track through the long narrow field opposite the house

15 Just before the end of the field bear L through bridlegate. At T-j with the road L then 1st track R by a red-brick house

◀ page 130

133

4 The Marriotts Way from Norwich to Reepham

Start

The Tourist Information Centre, the Guildhall, Market Square, Norwich

P There are car parks on Oak Street, off St Crispins, in the centre of Norwich. However, if arriving by car it might be better to consider starting in Drayton.

With little time spent on the traffic-filled streets of Norwich, and with cycle lanes and well-placed pelican crossings to help you negotiate the busy roads, it is possible to escape quickly and safely from the middle of the city to the heart of the countryside on a series of excellently maintained and well-signposted connecting trails that lead through Drayton and Lenwade to Reepham and, should one choose to link with off-road route 3, on to Aylsham and North Walsham, a total distance of 48 km (30 miles). It is surprising how close one passes to built-up areas and industrial estates while still maintaining the impression of being in a rural setting. The woodlands of Mileplain Plantation are a real delight: a deep cutting planted with sweet chestnut trees, especially attractive during the changing autumn colours. The whole route is studded with a wide variety of broadleaf trees – oak, ash, hawthorn, silver birch and sycamore. The clear, gently-flowing waters of the River Wensum are crossed three times on fine old metal bridges with wooden planking. Between Lenwade and Reepham you have the option of the full route following the Themelthorpe Loop or taking a shortcut which saves 6½ km (4 miles). The loop and shortcut could be made into a separate 11-km (7-mile) ride from Reepham and with route instructions in both directions (and the option of linking to off-road route 3) it should be possible to tailor a outing to suit your needs – from a short family ride right up to a 96-km (60-mile) challenge from Norwich to North Walsham and back again.

Norwich   6   7   9   4   A1067 20   Freeland Corner 45   25

0   5   10

Distance and grade

30 km (19 miles) one way Norwich–Lenwade –Themelthorpe–Reepham or 22 km (14 miles) using short-cut near Reepham

Moderate

Terrain

Easy, flat railway trail from the heart of the city through wooded cuttings and along embankments above arable land. Lowest point – 5m (16 feet) at the River Wensum in Norwich. Highest point – 50m (165 feet) at Themelthorpe

Nearest railway

Norwich

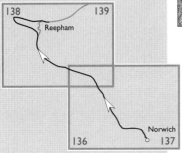

Places of interest

Norwich 1
See page 73

▲ The Marriotts Way near Reepham

Refreshments

Lots of choice in **Norwich**
Kings Arms PH ●, Old Brewery House PH ●, lots of choice in **Reepham**
Refreshments off the route in **Drayton** and **Lenwade**

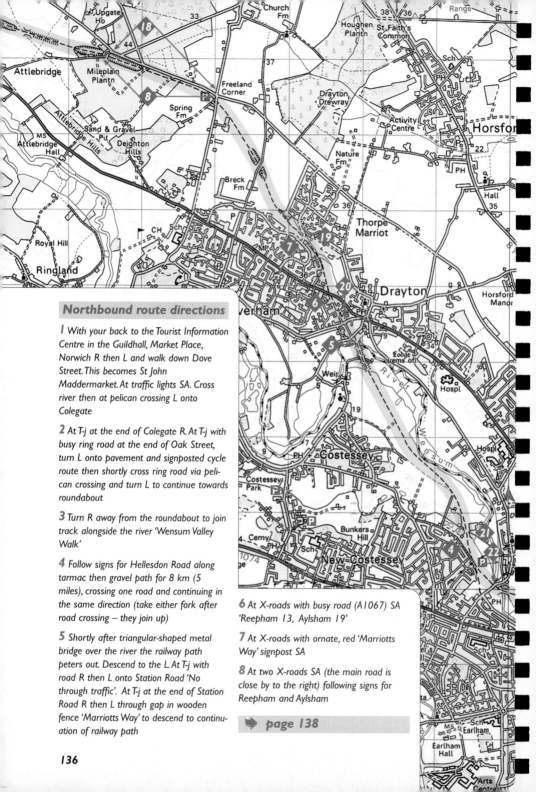

Northbound route directions

1 With your back to the Tourist Information Centre in the Guildhall, Market Place, Norwich R then L and walk down Dove Street. This becomes St John Maddermarket. At traffic lights SA. Cross river then at pelican crossing L onto Colegate

2 At T-j at the end of Colegate R. At T-j with busy ring road at the end of Oak Street, turn L onto pavement and signposted cycle route then shortly cross ring road via pelican crossing and turn L to continue towards roundabout

3 Turn R away from the roundabout to join track alongside the river 'Wensum Valley Walk'

4 Follow signs for Hellesdon Road along tarmac then gravel path for 8 km (5 miles), crossing one road and continuing in the same direction (take either fork after road crossing – they join up)

5 Shortly after triangular-shaped metal bridge over the river the railway path peters out. Descend to the L. At T-j with road R then L onto Station Road 'No through traffic'. At T-j at the end of Station Road R then L through gap in wooden fence 'Marriotts Way' to descend to continuation of railway path

6 At X-roads with busy road (A1067) SA 'Reepham 13, Aylsham 19'

7 At X-roads with ornate, red 'Marriotts Way' signpost SA

8 At two X-roads SA (the main road is close by to the right) following signs for Reepham and Aylsham

➡ *page 138*

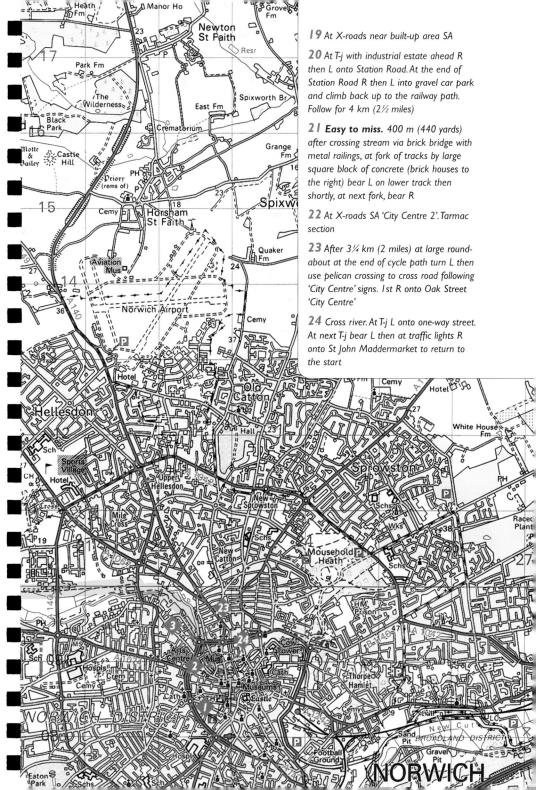

19 At X-roads near built-up area SA

20 At T-j with industrial estate ahead R then L onto Station Road. At the end of Station Road R then L into gravel car park and climb back up to the railway path. Follow for 4 km (2½ miles)

21 **Easy to miss.** 400 m (440 yards) after crossing stream via brick bridge with metal railings, at fork of tracks by large square block of concrete (brick houses to the right) bear L on lower track then shortly, at next fork, bear R

22 At X-roads SA 'City Centre 2'. Tarmac section

23 After 3¼ km (2 miles) at large round-about at the end of cycle path turn L then use pelican crossing to cross road following 'City Centre' signs. 1st R onto Oak Street 'City Centre'

24 Cross river. At T-j L onto one-way street. At next T-j bear L then at traffic lights R onto St John Maddermarket to return to the start

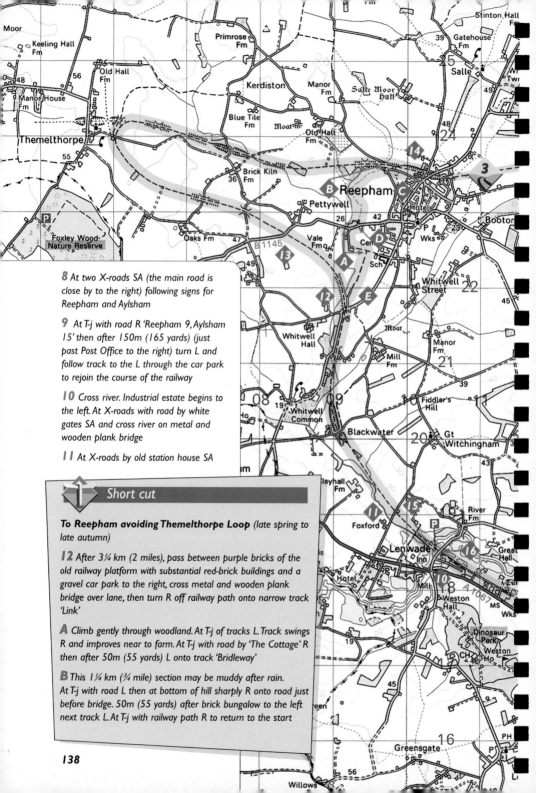

8 At two X-roads SA (the main road is close by to the right) following signs for Reepham and Aylsham

9 At T-j with road R 'Reepham 9, Aylsham 15' then after 150m (165 yards) (just past Post Office to the right) turn L and follow track to the L through the car park to rejoin the course of the railway

10 Cross river. Industrial estate begins to the left. At X-roads with road by white gates SA and cross river on metal and wooden plank bridge

11 At X-roads by old station house SA

Short cut

To Reepham avoiding Themelthorpe Loop *(late spring to late autumn)*

12 After 3¼ km (2 miles), pass between purple bricks of the old railway platform with substantial red-brick buildings and a gravel car park to the right, cross metal and wooden plank bridge over lane, then turn R off railway path onto narrow track 'Link'

A Climb gently through woodland. At T-j of tracks L. Track swings R and improves near to farm. At T-j with road by 'The Cottage' R then after 50m (55 yards) L onto track 'Bridleway'

B This 1¼ km (¾ mile) section may be muddy after rain. At T-j with road L then at bottom of hill sharply R onto road just before bridge. 50m (55 yards) after brick bungalow to the left next track L. At T-j with railway path R to return to the start

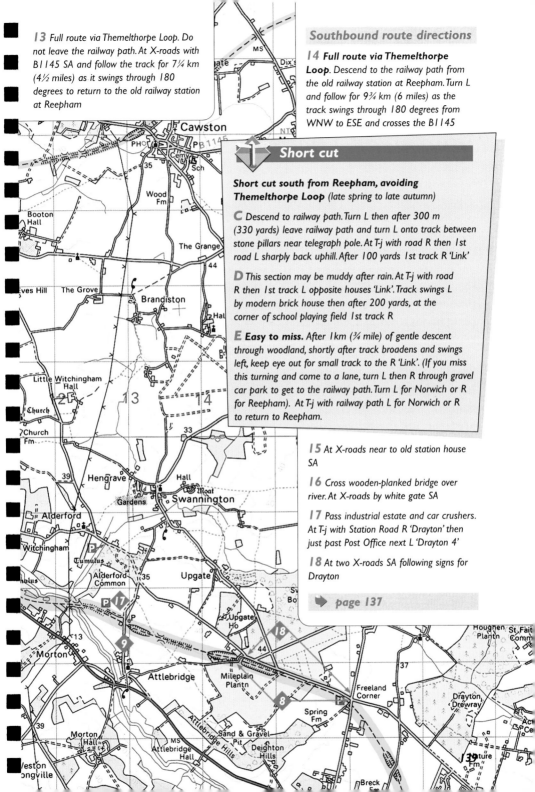

13 *Full route via Themelthorpe Loop. Do not leave the railway path. At X-roads with B1145 SA and follow the track for 7¼ km (4½ miles) as it swings through 180 degrees to return to the old railway station at Reepham*

14 **Full route via Themelthorpe Loop**. *Descend to the railway path from the old railway station at Reepham. Turn L and follow for 9¾ km (6 miles) as the track swings through 180 degrees from WNW to ESE and crosses the B1145*

Short cut

Short cut south from Reepham, avoiding Themelthorpe Loop *(late spring to late autumn)*

C *Descend to railway path. Turn L then after 300 m (330 yards) leave railway path and turn L onto track between stone pillars near telegraph pole. At T-j with road R then 1st road L sharply back uphill. After 100 yards 1st track R 'Link'*

D *This section may be muddy after rain. At T-j with road R then 1st track L opposite houses 'Link'. Track swings L by modern brick house then after 200 yards, at the corner of school playing field 1st track R*

E **Easy to miss.** *After 1km (¾ mile) of gentle descent through woodland, shortly after track broadens and swings left, keep eye out for small track to the R 'Link'. (If you miss this turning and come to a lane, turn L then R through gravel car park to get to the railway path. Turn L for Norwich or R for Reepham). At T-j with railway path L for Norwich or R to return to Reepham.*

15 *At X-roads near to old station house SA*

16 *Cross wooden-planked bridge over river. At X-roads by white gate SA*

17 *Pass industrial estate and car crushers. At T-j with Station Road R 'Drayton' then just past Post Office next L 'Drayton 4'*

18 *At two X-roads SA following signs for Drayton*

➡ *page 137*

5 Two waymarked forest routes on the Forestry Commission land near Thetford

Draw a line 16km (9 miles) around Thetford and you have some of the most consistently rideable offroad tracks in all of East Anglia: the soil has a sandy base and drains well and as the land is not good enough for farming, most of it is owned by the Forestry Commission and planted with pine trees. The forestry tracks around the plantations tend to have excellent all-year round surfaces and it is possible to devise any number of loops using these tracks. However, as is the case with all forestry land, it is almost impossible to give detailed route instructions when the only landmarks are trees and more trees, so the rides described are those that the Forestry Commision has already waymarked.

Start

High Lodge, on the Forest Drive south of the B1107 between Brandon and Thetford. OS National Grid reference TL811852

P As above

Distance and grade

20km (13 miles) in two loops, each of 10km (6½ miles)

Easy

Terrain

Well-waymarked tracks along sand and gravel tracks through conifer plantations. No hills.

Nearest railway

Brandon, 5 km (3 miles) north of the route at 5

Route instructions are given as a back-up to avoid getting lost. Even so, it is no bad idea to carry a compass with you so that you know in which direction you are travelling. Getting lost in Thetford Forest is hardly a life-threatening experience: you are never more than 3 km (2 miles) from a road, so if you do lose your way either retrace your steps to where you last knew where you were or continue in a straight line until you find a road and you should soon be able to re-orientate yourself.

Downham Highlodge Warren

High Wrong Corner

Mayday Farm

34   42

1·5

0   5   10

Brandon *5 km (3 miles) west of the start*
A town much admired for its buildings made of flint from
local mines. There is an excellent example of flint and red
brickwork on the 18th-century Brandon Hall

 Refreshments

*Teas and coffees at the **Visitor Centre***
*Lots of choice in **Brandon** and*
Thetford

Thetford *5 km (3 miles) southeast
of the start*
The East Anglian capital of the
Danes in the 9th century. There are
extensive ruins of the 12th-century
priory. Castle Hill has Iron Age earth-
works and a Norman castle mound.
The church is part Saxon, part
Norman. There are medieval and Georgian buildings in
almost every street. The 15th-century Ancient House
houses the local and natural history museum

Grime's Graves *4½ km (3 miles) north of the start*
Visitors can descend about 10m (30 ft), by ladder, into an
excavated shaft of these Neolithic flint mines and look
along the radiating galleries from which the flint for making
knives and
axes was
extracted.
The site is
unique in
England and
comprises
more than 300
pits and shafts

▼ *Thetford Priory*

▲ Grime's Graves

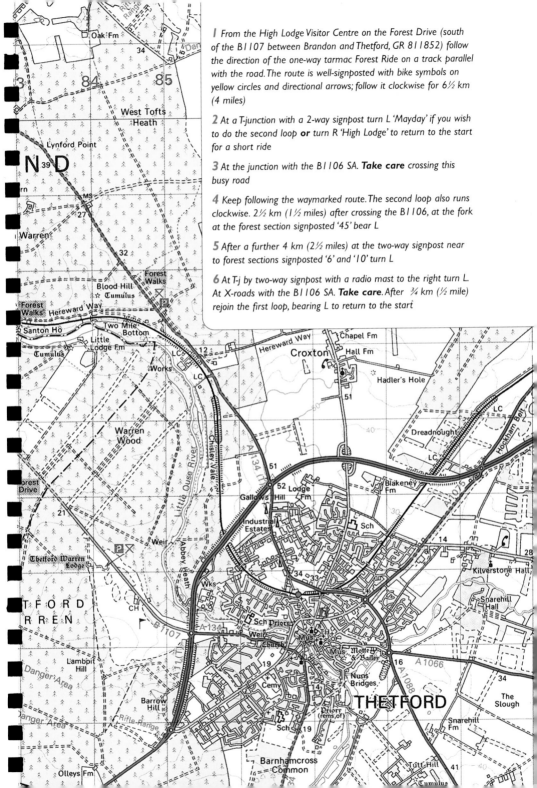

1 *From the High Lodge Visitor Centre on the Forest Drive (south of the B1107 between Brandon and Thetford, GR 811852) follow the direction of the one-way tarmac Forest Ride on a track parallel with the road. The route is well-signposted with bike symbols on yellow circles and directional arrows; follow it clockwise for 6½ km (4 miles)*

2 *At a T-junction with a 2-way signpost turn L 'Mayday' if you wish to do the second loop **or** turn R 'High Lodge' to return to the start for a short ride*

3 *At the junction with the B1106 SA. **Take care** crossing this busy road*

4 *Keep following the waymarked route. The second loop also runs clockwise. 2½ km (1½ miles) after crossing the B1106, at the fork at the forest section signposted '45' bear L*

5 *After a further 4 km (2½ miles) at the two-way signpost near to forest sections signposted '6' and '10' turn L*

6 *At T-j by two-way signpost with a radio mast to the right turn L. At X-roads with the B1106 SA. **Take care**. After ¾ km (½ mile) rejoin the first loop, bearing L to return to the start*

Ordnance Survey Cycle TOURS ORDER FORM

*T*he whole series is available from all good bookshops or by mail order direct from the publisher (**free** postage and packing). Payment can be made by credit card or cheque/postal order in the following ways:

By phone Phone your order through on our special *Credit Card Hotline* on *01933 443863 (Fax: 01933 443849)*. Speak to our customer service team during office hours (9am to 5pm) or leave a message on the answer machine, quoting your full credit card number plus expiry date and your full name and address and reference.

By post Simply fill out the order form (you may photocopy it) and send it to: *Philip's Direct, 27 Sanders Road, Wellingborough, Northants NN8 4NL.*

I wish to order the following titles	Quantity @ £9.99 each	£ Total
AROUND BIRMINGHAM	0 600 58623 5 ➤	
AROUND LONDON	0 600 58845 9 ➤	
AVON, SOMERSET & WILTSHIRE	0 600 58664 2 ➤	
BERKS, BUCKS & OXFORDSHIRE	0 600 58156 X ➤	
CENTRAL SCOTLAND	0 600 59005 4 ➤	
CORNWALL & DEVON	0 600 58124 1 ➤	
CUMBRIA & THE LAKES	0 600 58126 8 ➤	
DORSET, HAMPSHIRE & ISLE OF WIGHT	0 600 58667 7 ➤	
EAST ANGLIA – NORTH	0 600 59219 7 ➤	
EAST ANGLIA – SOUTH	0 600 58125 X ➤	
GLOUCESTERSHIRE & HEREFORD & WORCESTER	0 600 58665 0 ➤	
KENT, SURREY & SUSSEX	0 600 58666 9 ➤	
NORTH WALES & THE MARCHES	0 600 59007 0 ➤	
NORTH YORKSHIRE & TEESSIDE	0 600 59103 4 ➤	
NORTHUMBERLAND & COUNTY DURHAM	0 600 59105 0 ➤	
PEAK DISTRICT	0 600 58889 0 ➤	
SOUTHERN SCOTLAND	0 600 58624 3 ➤	
SOUTH, WEST & MID-WALES	0 600 58846 7 ➤	
YORKSHIRE DALES	0 600 58847 5 ➤	

Name..

Address...

....

....Postcode

◆ **Free postage and packing**
◆ All available titles will normally be dispatched within 5 working days of receipt of order but please allow up to 28 days for delivery
◆ Whilst every effort is made to keep prices low, the publisher reserves the right to increase prices at short notice
☐ Please tick this box if you do not wish your name to be used by other carefully selected organisations that may wish to send you information about other products and services

Registered Office: 25 Victoria Street, London SW1H 0EX
Registered in England number: 3396524

I enclose a cheque/postal order, for a **total** of

made payable to *Reed Book Services*, or please debit my

☐ Access ☐ American Express ☐ Visa ☐ Diners

account by

Account no ☐☐☐☐ ☐☐☐☐ ☐☐☐☐ ☐☐☐☐

Expiry date ☐☐ ☐☐

Signature...

Post to: Philip's Direct, 27 Sanders Road, Wellingborough, Northants NN8 4NL